# RAMBAM

by Rochel Yaffe

illustrated by Norman Nodel

Hachai
PUBLISHING

# RAMBAM
## The Story of
## Rabbi Moshe Ben Maimon

FIRST EDITION
First Impression - JUNE 1992
Revised POD edition - 2014

**Editor:** D. L. Rosenfeld
**Layout:** Moshe Cohen


LCCN 9322265
ISBN 978-1-929628-81-0 (Revised POD edition)
ISBN 978-0-922613-14-4 (Original Hardcover edition)
ISBN 978-0-922613-15-1 (Original softcover edition)


**HACHAI PUBLISHING**
Brooklyn, N.Y.
Tel: 718-633-0100 - Fax: 718-633-0103
www.hachai.com - info@hachai.com

# Contents

ATLANTIC OCEAN

FRANCE

SPAIN

PORTUGAL

★ TOLEDO

CORDOVA

ITALY

TUNISIA

FEZ ★

MOROCCO

ALGERIA

M

LI

1. **CORDOVA** – Birthplace of the Rambam

2. **TOLEDO** ⎫

3. **FEZ** ⎬ – Cities to which the Rambam and

⎭       his family fled to escape persecution

4. CAIRO — The capital of Egypt where the Rambam served as the Caliph's personal physician

5. TIBERIAS — The Rambam's place of burial

In that era (of Mashiach) there will be neither famine nor war, neither envy nor competition, for good things will flow in abundance and all the delights will be as freely available as dust. The occupation of the entire world will be soley to know G-d; as it is written, (Yeshayahu 11:9), "For the world will be filled with the knowledge of G-d as the waters cover the ocean bed."

Rabbi Moshe Ben Maimon
Mishneh Torah Sefer Shoftim
Hilchos Melochim 12:5

## Prologue

The silence in the room hung heavily in the air as Rav Yehudah HaCohen shuffled through the papers. "The Ravad... aah, Rabbi Avraham ben David." He lifted the stack of credentials and returned them to his visitor. "With this I am satisfied. We know we can trust you. But secrecy is of the essence. Not a word to anyone."

Benyamin nodded vigorously. "G-d forbid that I should endanger the life of my friend."

Rav Yehudah regarded him soberly. In a hushed voice he instructed, "Tomorrow a few students are going to visit him in his hiding place. Be outside the yeshiva after *Maariv*."

Benyamin rose, elated. He shook hands warmly with the dignified rabbi. "Thank you, thank you! You don't know what this means to me... after all these years."

The rabbi only nodded and laid a finger on his lips.

Two students were waiting for him the next evening in the black shadow of the yeshiva building. He followed them as they strode through the darkened side streets leading to the outskirts of town.

They began to climb into the foothills outside of the city. The moon floated above the peaks, casting a pale sheen upon the path. Black masses of shadows lay all around them. The path grew steeper and then disappeared. The boys moved swiftly and surely, comfortably familiar with the trek.

Suddenly they halted. Benyamin glanced at his young guides in surprise. He saw nothing before him, only a rocky projection in the hillside, dimly illuminated by the glow of the moon. The boys peered sharply around them, then rapped several times loudly on the rock.

What was this? Benyamin wondered. Some secret, underground path to the Rambam's hiding place? Dumbly he watched as the students bent down, and with a sharp, scraping sound, pushed a boulder from the side of the cliff.

Benyamin instinctively stepped back when confronted with the intense, blinding light streaming out of the opening in the mountain. Then, blinking in amazement, he beheld the most awesome sight he had ever seen.

He was staring into a cave brightly lit by several tall, yellow wax tapers fixed to the veined rock wall. Behind a large desk strewn with rolls of parchment, sat a Jew with a holy face that was framed by a silver beard. His entire being seemed to glow with some mysterious inner light.

For a wild moment, Benyamin thought he had stumbled

upon the cave of the holy Rashbi, who had hidden from the Roman conquerors more than a thousand years ago.

The Rav behind the desk recognized him immediately. He rose with a kindly, welcoming smile and advanced toward his visitor with outstretched arms, crying, "Benyamin – from Toledo!"

It was then that the man realized that this rabbi was none other than his childhood companion Moshe, whom he had come to seek. But never again would he – could he – refer to his old friend in so familiar a manner.

## Chapter One

# THE RUNAWAY

Moshe was not looking into his *siddur* again. He was standing next to his father and brother by the eastern wall of the synagogue. It was a place of honor, for Moshe's father was the Jewish judge, *dayan*, of Cordova, just as his grandfather had been before him.

The small boy's eyes wandered over the intricate arabesques decorating the wall. The designs had been carved into the plaster, his father had told him, and then painted with brilliant colors. For the hundredth time, Moshe tried to decipher the letters of gold that stood out in bold relief against the rich background.

"M-i-k-d-a-s-h M'-a-t..."

Miniature Temple.

Moshe knew what the words meant: that ever since the destruction of the *Beit HaMikdash*, the synagogues stood in its place.

He felt a sharp tap on his shoulder and looked up guiltily. His father, wrapped in a *tallit*, was regarding him with his penetrating gaze. The gray eyes beneath the heavy brows were stern as usual, but lately Moshe had seen something else in his father's expression. It was a look of disappointment, of sadness, which troubled Moshe more than the anger. Moshe knew that he was the cause of his father's sadness. He, the eldest son, a direct descendent of Rabbi Yehuda HaNasi, could not learn Torah. He could not keep his eyes on the shiny black letters that marched across the parchment. Like the wrought-iron gate in front of their house, the letters seemed to form a barrier, saying, "Keep out. You cannot enter."

His little brother David, so much younger, had no trouble following the *tefillot*. He stood beside Moshe, his curly head bent intently over the *siddur*, singing along with the congregation in a high, sweet voice, not missing a word.

*Why am I so different?* Moshe wondered despondently. *Why is it that no matter how hard I try, the letters will not yield their meaning to me?* Grown men would wait in another room to ask his father's advice or to have their disputes settled, to be taught how to live by the Torah. But he allowed them to wait while he spent precious hours going over the Chumash again and again with Moshe, pleading, "Look inside, Moshe. Just follow where I am reading."

As the lesson progressed, his father's patient voice would become tighter, sharper, until Moshe would finally be dismissed with a sigh and a shake of the head.

Only a few days ago, Moshe had slipped out of the sunny study, his face hot with shame, his eyes stinging with unshed tears. He had wandered into the clean kitchen where Batsheva was busy over the fire. The room smelled of rose petal jam and honey cake. The housekeeper, flushed from the heat of the fire, slipped a cake into his open palm.

"Didn't it go well today?" she asked him sympathetically. "Is your father upset at you again?"

Moshe shook his head, unable to speak.

"Well, you know how it is, Moshe." Batsheva dropped rings of batter into a pot of boiling oil. "Seven generations of scholars... it is little wonder he expects you to follow in their footsteps. An unbroken chain of *dayanim*..."

"I guess David will have to be the *dayan*. He already knows the Chumash better than I. Why, Batsheva," he asked plaintively, "why am I different?"

"Well, Moshe," the housekeeper replied, regarding him with her kind, shrewd eyes, "not everyone is cut out to be a scholar. Maybe you take after the other side of your family..."

"You mean, after my mother's father... the butcher," said Moshe, vaguely ashamed.

"There is no need to be ashamed of your grandfather. I knew him well. It is true that he was a simple Jew, but it would be hard to find a kinder, straighter, more generous man. And G-d-fearing! If he had the slightest doubt about an animal's *kashrut*, he would give it away to the Muslims. No, you have nothing to be ashamed of in your mother's family, may she rest in peace. It is little wonder that Hashem made the honorable match between your parents."

"I wonder –" Moshe began.

" You wonder why your father, the famous Rabbi Maimon, would take a wife from among such simple folk. Sit down, little one, and I will tell you the story. I'm surprised you haven't heard it before now."

Moshe listened, fascinated, as Batsheva told him of his father's dream. Rabbi Maimon had been over forty years old and still unmarried. His love for the Torah consumed every moment of the day, and he had never taken the time to look into the many fine matches that were offered to him. And then one night he had a dream. An old man, with a radiant face and a flowing white beard, appeared to him and told him sternly that it was time for him to marry.

"Go to the village near Cordova," he instructed, "and take the butcher's daughter for your bride." Rabbi Maimon tried to ignore the dream, but it was repeated night after night until Rabbi Maimon was convinced that the butcher's daughter was indeed his intended wife, ordained in heaven. He traveled to the town near Cordova and informed the astonished butcher that he had come to take his daughter for a wife.

"And they were wed..." Batsheva's voice trailed off as she allowed herself to be carried away with memories. "Your mother was a lovely girl, modest, kind. They were very happy until –"

"Until I was born," Moshe interrupted sadly.

"Yes, poor thing. I will never forget the day. The house was spanking clean. We had cooked and baked all week.

*Moshe listened, fascinated, as Batsheva told him of his father's dream.*

Everything was ready for the Seder. And your poor father, pacing up and down, never stopped whispering *Tehillim*. For a day and a night, your mother struggled. At last – I'll never forget it – on the afternoon of *Erev* Pesach of the year 4895, we heard the cry of a baby. That was you, Moshe. And your dear mother returned her pure soul to G-d."

"They laid you in my arms, a little baby yelling loudly for his mother. Your father trusted me to care for you. He had known our family for many years."

Batsheva rose and with quick, expert movements, scooped the golden balls of dough out of the oil and piled them on a platter. "And even after your father remarried and your brother and sister were born, I always felt that you were my special boy."

Moshe had left the room with another honey cake, and a warm, happy feeling in his heart.

The congregation rose to recite *Shemonah Esrei*.

Coming out of his daydream, Moshe found the right page and cast a sidelong glance at his father. Had he noticed that Moshe's attention had strayed?

He bent his head in prayer. The words sprang up at him from the page: *"Grant us wisdom, understanding and knowledge."*

"Wisdom, understanding, knowledge..." Moshe whispered the words fervently. Perhaps today's lesson would be different.

Perhaps Hashem would grant him wisdom and understanding, and he would remember every word his father taught him. Then his father's grave face would crease into a smile, and his eyes would be filled with pride instead of sadness.

From now on, Moshe resolved, he would really try much harder. On the way home from the *beit k'nesset*, he took care to walk sedately beside his father instead of loitering behind to examine a caterpillar rippling across a leaf or to observe a bird in flight. The streets were crowded with Jews strolling homeward, their *tallitot* draped over their shoulders. Turbaned Moors and heavily veiled women passed by them. No one bothered the Jews. Moshe's father often reminded him to thank G-d for granting peace and tranquility to the Jewish people in Cordova. Here, at least, Jews could serve Hashem openly and free of fear.

Not long after breakfast Rabbi Maimon called, "Come, Moshe. Let's learn a little Chumash." Carefully, Rabbi Maimon unrolled a small Torah scroll and laid it lovingly on the table. "Do you want to review?" he asked Moshe. "Or should I repeat yesterday's lesson?"

"Can you say it just one more time, Father?"

His father nodded and began. *"And the earth was empty and void, and there was darkness on the face of the deep, and the spirit of Hashem hovered over the water. And G-d said, 'Let there be light,' and there was light."*

Moshe tried to imagine how the world had looked when nothing existed. Through the open window, he saw his own familiar world, bright in the morning light. The fountain glistened in the sun, murmuring over its basin. Palm and myrtle trees swayed on the patio, dappling the tiled floor with shade. The brilliant bougainvillea, like so many butterflies, lifted their faces to the sun.

"Moshe!" His father's voice cracked like a whip. "Look inside! Can't you at least look in? Even if you don't understand, at least connect your eyes with the holy letters!"

Moshe shook his head miserably. "I can't!"

"I don't want to hear that. You can't because you won't! You can't because you don't try! I hung onto every word of my rebbe, Rabbi Yosef Ibn Migash, his every gesture, when I was young. His father rose, towering over him in anger. "All you care about is your foolishness. Go, then, go and play. Get out of my sight, you... you son of a butcher! I don't want to see you!"

For a moment Moshe stood transfixed, as if his father's words were a spear that had pierced him through and pinned him to his seat. And then he was running, running through the sun-dappled balcony and out of the wrought iron gate. His feet clattered on the brick-paved streets, but they did not drown out the terrible words: "Go, out of my sight... son of a butcher... son of a butcher..."

He ran past a row of lime-washed houses and through the marketplace, crowded with fruit and vegetable stands. At last he

*"Get out of my sight, you... you son of a butcher!"*

found himself on the outskirts of the town, where the river ran like a gray silk ribbon. Over lush fields and meadows he ran until he reached the riverbank.

Burning all over, Moshe stripped off his linen coat and threw himself into the cold, clear water, reaching out with strong strokes. The cool waves closed in around him soothingly. Moshe was a strong swimmer. His father had taught him, explaining that a father is obligated to teach his son how to learn Torah, how to earn a living, and how to swim. "So far," Moshe thought, "I have only learned to swim."

At last he dropped onto the riverbank, exhausted. No one owned this land, so feeling a pang of hunger, Moshe reached for a pomegranate and peeled it open. Reciting the appropriate bracha, he sucked the sweet juice around the kernels hungrily. Yes, he would stay here, living on the plentiful fruit of the river bank, and would never go back to face his father.

Moshe awoke with a start some time later, to behold a sky of rose-red clouds. The setting sun glistened behind them, transforming the river into a glittering band of gold. Suddenly, all the color had passed from the sky, and the stars were shining. In the distance, Moshe heard the mournful bark of a stray dog. He stood up, undecided. Where should he go? He could sneak back quietly to the safety of the house and tiptoe up to his room, where little David would be stretched out on the bed, already asleep. But his father had driven him from the house. *"Get out of my sight, you son of a butcher!"*

Lost in thought, Moshe found himself in front of the high, wide facade of the *beit k'nesset.* His feet had carried him to the one spot where everyone was welcome. The wings of the building seemed to beckon him inside. Moshe clambered up a tree branch and looked in through a window. The sanctuary was empty, the hanging lamp over the aron kodesh bathing the long room in a soft light. Moshe opened the heavy wooden door and slipped inside.

He found himself standing in front of the aron, crafted of the finest burnished cedar wood from Mount Hermon, in the Holy Land. Something made him reach out and open the carved doors. He caught his breath.

In the shadowy depths of the ark, the Torah scrolls sparkled and glistened in their silver mantles. Suddenly, the cold, hard knot inside his chest loosened, and a flood of tears cooled his cheeks. "Please, Hashem," he whispered, "give me wisdom. Open my head. Let me understand Your holy Torah so that my father can be proud of me. Then my mother will look down from *Gan Eden* and see that she did not give her life for nothing. Please, please teach me Your Torah."

A feeling of peace swept over Moshe. One by one he kissed the glowing scrolls and carefully closed the doors of the ark. He recited the *Shema*, curled up on one of the benches that lined the wall, and was soon fast asleep.

## Chapter Two

# OFF TO YESHIVA

Dawn was turning the windows a bright yellow as Moshe awoke with a start. His eyes rested on the vaulted ceiling of the *beit k'nesset*, and the events of the previous day came flooding back. Had he really run away from home and spent the night in the synagogue? He recalled the moment when he had stood before the ark, when the glorious silver Torahs seemed to nod to him in encouragement, and he felt again the great peace that had followed his prayer. He murmured *Modeh Ani*, all the while contemplating what he should do. Moshe decided to go to Alisena. There he would learn Torah from the great Rabbi Yosef Ign Migash, his father's teacher. How often he had heard his father quote the great rabbi while speaking publicly in this very synagogue! Yes, that is where he would go. He would study with all his might. And when he returned, he would tell his father all that Rabbi Yosef had taught him.

Moshe washed his hands and recited *Shacharit* in the silent synagogue. He kissed the mezuza and ran, lightfooted, to the marketplace. The large square was already filling up as farmers began to unload their baskets, heaped high with pimentos, lettuce, figs, dates, and grapes. A sudden hollow feeling in his stomach reminded Moshe that he had eaten only a pomegranate since the previous morning. He turned his eyes from the tempting display and caught sight of a Jewish farmer who was loading his cart with empty baskets as the donkeys stood patiently by, swatting at flies with their tails.

"Sir, can you tell me how to get to Alisena?" called Moshe.

The sun-darkened man smiled at him. "Why, son, that is just where I am headed – back to Alisena. I've sold everything, *Baruch Hashem*, so it's time to go home. You're going to the yeshiva, I suppose." He scrutinized Moshe's appearance approvingly. "I took one look at you and thought, that is a little scholar!"

"Yes, that's exactly what I intend to be, and that's exactly where I'm going!" Moshe exclaimed in delight.

"Hop up and have something to eat," called the farmer as he untied the donkeys from their post. He tossed a golden orange at Moshe.

Soon they were climbing the ruddy hills of Cordova. They turned a bend in the road, and Moshe saw the white city, nestled in cypress and myrtle, lying toward the south in the morning sun. A silver olive tree seemed to be waving its branches to him in farewell. "Good- bye," he whispered. "I will be back when I am a scholar, like Rabbi Akiva."

They traveled all day, and it was evening when the farmer pointed to the lights of Alisena. He stopped in front of a large, square building, brightly lit in spite of the late hour. "Here you are," the farmer said kindly. "Learn a lot of Torah and be a light to our people, little scholar." Moshe looked wistfully after the kind farmer until his wagon had disappeared around a curve in the road.

Moshe approached the door timidly. A few students were leaving, and through the open doorway Moshe saw rows of men and boys studying together. With a pang, he realized that they were all much older than he. Many were adults with full beards. Hesitantly, he knocked. A tall, young man came to the doorway, regarding him with a smile. "What do you want, little boy?"

Moshe's throat constricted and he stood mute. What was he doing here, a young boy, who had never even mastered a *pasuk* in Chumash, in this yeshiva of serious talmidim? At last he heard his voice stammering, "I... I came to learn Torah with Rabbi Yosef Ibn Migash."

"To study Torah with my father?" the young man chuckled. "You have chosen well. Come back when you are a bar mitzva, and we will make you a scholar. But right now, you'd better go home to your mother. It's getting late, and she will be worrying about you."

Moshe felt the world crashing in around him. "But I can't!" he cried desperately. "I can't go home. I must stay here and learn Torah." To his dismay, he burst into tears. "Please, please let me speak to Rabbi Yosef."

Several students were standing around him now. "Hush," said one. "Rabbi Yosef is giving a *shiur*. Be off, boy." He started to close the door, but then, all at once, the chanting of the students ceased.

"Bring the boy to me," someone demanded. The voice was mild but held an undeniable authority. "Let me see him."

A path opened in the center of the long hall. The students parted sharply to allow Moshe to walk to the head of the room, where a man with a silver beard was sitting. Moshe looked into his eyes, eyes that were as deep and as wide as the ocean. The young boy could not tear his gaze from them.

"What is your name, my son?" the rabbi asked in a voice full of kindness.

Suddenly Moshe was no longer afraid. "I am Moshe, the son of Maimon from Cordova."

"Ah, Maimon, my student!" The holy face bent toward him attentively. "And your father has sent you to learn Torah in this yeshiva?"

The students pressed closer.

"No, Rebbe." Moshe hung his head. "He did not send me. I... I came on my own."

After that it was easy. Moshe's story came out in a rush: how he had never been able to study Torah, how his father had sent him away, the wonderful change that had come over him when he stood in front of the aron kodesh. "Please, Rebbe, please teach me Torah, as you taught my father."

Moshe felt the lips of the *tzaddik* on his forehead, and he heard these words: "May Hashem bless you, my son." At that moment he felt as if a heavy weight had been lifted from his shoulders. Something opened up inside, something deep and good. (In later years he would say that it was at this moment that the wells of wisdom were revealed to him.)

The next morning, Rabbi Yosef Ibn Migash sat down with Moshe and began to teach him. Moshe bent toward the scroll with great eagerness, without a trace of his old fear. And behold, the black letters, which had formerly seemed to be a chain of iron rails, parted and welcomed him into the parlor of Torah. And the words that had once been dense and opaque became translucent as glass.

*"And Hashem said, let there be light,"* read Rabbi Yosef, *"and there was light. And G-d saw that the light was good, and He divided between the light and the darkness."* He paused and asked his young charge, "But how could this be possible, Moshe? Didn't Hashem wait until the fourth day, when He had created the sun and the moon, to separate light and darkness, day and night? Why then is it written here, on the first day?"

"This must have been a different kind of light," said Moshe, wrinkling his brow. "It must have been a light that was created before the sun and the moon."

"Well spoken, Moshe." Rabbi Yosef nodded his silver head. "It was a different sort of light, higher and purer from that of the sun and the moon. It was a light so pure and holy and penetrating that Hashem took it and saved it for the *tzaddikim* in the World to Come. He has concealed it in the words of Torah."

"And whoever studies the holy Torah..." began Moshe.

"...draws down this holy light into his soul and into the world around him. How fortunate we are, Moshe! How good is our portion, how pleasant is our lot, to be the people whom Hashem chose to receive His Torah!"

Then, much too soon, Rabbi Yosef rose. "Now go and review, my child, learn with all the fire of your warm heart and the clarity of your brain, and you will go from strength to strength. I will send word to your father about your progress."

And Moshe did learn, from early morning to late at night, until the last candle burned out. He had been granted wings to soar through the books of the Chumash, the Mishna, and the Gemara. Every day brought new discoveries, revealed new layers of meaning in each word, each letter.

He, who had not been able to concentrate for more than a minute, had to be reminded to eat and drink, to stretch his legs, to sleep so that he would have strength for the morning.

"You have made my father very happy," Meir told Moshe one evening.

"How... how do you know?" Moshe asked, his breath catching joyfully in his throat.

"Listen to what he said about you last night. Meir closed his eyes to remember the exact words. 'Hear, my sons, and know, that this boy will become a great man. The Jewish People will walk by his light from the rising of the sun to its setting.'"

Then, without warning, it all ended. Rabbi Yosef's seat stood empty and desolate at the head of the table. The long room no longer rang with the joyous sounds of Torah. Gone was the happy chant, the exuberant give-and-take of discussion and argument. A heavy silence hung over the room, broken only by the subdued murmuring of students reciting *Tehillim*, praying for their beloved teacher who was so ill.

Finally, one morning, on a street thronged with silent Jews, a simple wooden box was borne on the shoulders of the weeping students. Rabbi Yosef was gone.

For Moshe, the yeshiva was no longer what it had been. At every turn, at every corner, he expected to see the beloved face framed by the flowing beard, the luminous eyes, the head bent attentively toward his students. When the seven days of shiva were over, Moshe stood gazing at the dusty road that led across the brick-red hills to Cordova. He knew what he must do.

*Shacharit* had just ended. The congregation of the Great Synagogue of Cordova turned toward the aron, awaiting the reading of the Torah. It was at this moment that a slender youth slipped out of the shadows and walked purposefully toward the podium. He banged the stand twice for attention. The sound echoed loudly in the high-ceilinged chamber.

He began to speak about the parsha of the week, his eyes fixed on the silk cloth before him. His voice grew stronger as he repeated the holy words of his rebbe, Rabbi Yosef Ibn Migash. His eyes swept the long room as he shared with the people of his city the brilliant Torah thoughts of his teacher.

"All this," he concluded in a firm, clear voice, "and much more I learned from our teacher, Rabbi Yosef Ibn Migash, *zecher tzaddik livracha*. May he rest in peace and may his merit protect us."

When he finished, there was a moment of silence before the burst of approval came from the congregants.

"Excellent."

"A well of living water."

"Isn't he the son of Rabbi Maimon?"

"An apple doesn't fall far from the tree."

Moshe had turned to run from the podium, overwhelmed with the daring of what he had done, when he was suddenly enfolded in a pair of strong arms. The beloved face he had seen in his mind every day during his sojourn in Alisena was pressed against his own, and he felt his father's hot tears and heard him whisper, "Forgive me, my son, forgive me."

They walked home together. David, taller and thinner, held Moshe tightly by the hand. "I knew you would come back, Moshe, I knew it. I prayed every night that you would come home."

They spoke of many things as they strolled through the sunlit streets of Cordova. David begged to know every detail of

*"Forgive me, my son, forgive me."*

Moshe's adventure. His father entreated him to recall each word Rabbi Yosef had said to him. They spoke sadly of the passing of the great *tzaddik* and the vacuum he had left behind. Finally they reached the house, comfortably shaded by a towering cypress tree. Moshe's stepmother, little sister, and Batsheva had all heard the news and were running toward him.

Rabbi Maimon gathered his family around him. His strong, confident voice was quiet and thoughtful. "I did an unforgivable thing. In my anger, I drove my own dear son out of my home. But our Father in heaven did not desert him. He led him down the true path to the house of G-d." And then, more cheerfully, he announced, "Moshe and David – tomorrow, we will start learning together."

## Chapter Three

# FLIGHT

This is the view of *Beit Hillel,* "Rabbi Maimon chanted while swaying over the Gemara. "But *Beit Shammai* disagrees. Let us see where the difference lies." Free for the moment from the cares of the community, Rabbi Maimon was enjoying his daily learning session with his two sons. Sunlight streamed in through the window of the study and illuminated his strong face. The deep furrows in his forehead softened during these precious times, and his gray eyes glowed with fatherly pride in the progress of his children.

"I am sorry to interrupt you," came their mother's voice, strained and anxious. "But there is a man here, a refugee, I think. He looks terrible but won't eat or drink anything. He says he's here on urgent business and insists on seeing you right away."

Rabbi Maimon nodded, and the visitor entered and leaned against the whitewashed wall of the study as if he were too spent to stand. Moshe's first thought was that he had never seen anyone so thin, not even the blind Muslim beggars who sat cross-legged in the marketplace. His skin was brown as a nut and stretched tightly over his bones. His caftan, worn to shreds, was held together by an odd assortment of strings and rags. Blood stained the tattered cloth that swathed his feet.

"Do you know me, Rabbi Maimon?" he asked in a dry, cracked voice that was hardly above a whisper. "I am Yonatan. We learned together in Alisena."

Rabbi Maimon froze for a moment, then hurried to his old friend, placing both hands on the living skeleton's shoulders and staring into his face. "Yonatan, Yonatan! What has happened to you?"

"Alisena is gone. The yeshiva, the the *beit k'nesset*, the holy sefarim... ashes, a heap of ashes."

The man sank into a seat. The family regarded him in silence; then, of one accord, they breathed, "The Almohades."

"They stormed the city in two days." The man's black eyes seemed to sink deeper into his shriveled cheekbones as he told the story. "They overran the Jewish Quarter, thousands of them, brandishing their weapons, shouting, 'Allah or the sword!' We were given three days to leave the city. My wife... she had just given birth... she was weak... the baby was too small. We couldn't go. Others stayed because of elderly parents, illness, fear. They rounded us up, beating us into the marketplace. They kept shouting, 'Allah or the sword!' We were given a choice. We could say the words they demanded – 'Allah is the Lord and Mohammed is his prophet' – or die. Many turned their faces from us and proclaimed what they were ordered to proclaim." The man fell silent, staring straight ahead, lost in the terrible vision.

"And the others?" Rabbi Maimon asked.

"They were slaughtered – old men and women, young

"They rounded us up, beating us into the marketplace.
they kept shouting, 'Allah or the sword!'"

brides, little children... my children. Their last words were... *Shema Yisrael.*" The man bent his face into his hands and wept.

The sound of tearing cloth pierced the room. Rabbi Maimon had rent his caftan. "Blessed is the true Judge," he whispered, and his sons said, "Amen."

"Rabbi Maimon, I am here to warn you." The man rose, leaning heavily on the table. "I must have fainted when they slashed my neck, but they didn't kill me. I awoke, lying among the bodies in the square. The tiles were sticky with blood. If my life was saved, it was for this."

He leaned forward and gripped Rabbi Maimon's hand with his own thin claws. "You must flee at once, and so must all the Jews who are able to run. The Muslims are busy now, smashing, pillaging, destroying. But soon they will be here. Malaga and Granada have already fallen."

"But where, Yonatan, where can we go?"

"You must go over the mountains. Hire a guide and take along food and warm blankets. Travel by night. Go north, to Toledo. Alfonso the Seventh is admitting Jews to the city. He himself is a Christian and hates the Muslims. Save yourself, Rabbi Maimon. Your flock needs a shepherd."

Their mother returned, carrying a steaming cup of tea and a bowl of hot soup. The man took the drink, but waved away the soup. "I must go farther. The people must be warned." He pushed the door open.

Rabbi Maimon and his wife pleaded with the refugee to

rest for a day or two, assuring him that they would send messengers to all the neighboring towns to repeat his words. But he would not hear of it. "I myself must warn them. Why else would G-d have spared me?" He was persuaded to change his rags for a clean caftan of Rabbi Maimon's, which hung loosely on his emaciated frame, and a sturdy pair of shoes. Then, as suddenly as he had come, he was gone.

The family sat numbly, too stunned to speak.

At last they heard Rabbi Maimon murmur, "What tragedy, what destruction! Oh, Master of the Universe, the yeshiva, my friends! What will become of Your children? What will become of Your Torah?"

"Father," Moshe said, touching Rabbi Maimon's arm, "the man warned us that we must hurry. Shouldn't we do as he said?"

Rabbi Maimon roused himself. "Yes, yes, it is a mitzva to guard one's life. We must pack, we must prepare for the journey..."

Their mother rose, her face pale but composed. "Batsheva and I will begin to pack clothing and linens and food. We will have to take along dried figs and beans." She looked around at the shelves piled high with scrolls, and a ghost of a smile touched her lips. "This will be the hardest part. You'll have to decide which sefarim to carry." She hurried out, holding her little daughter tightly by the hand.

"We will have to take at least one *Sefer Torah*," said David.

"And the Gemara we were studying," added Moshe.

"And Father, please don't forget the notes you took when you were listening to Rabbi Yosef Ibn Migash..."

"And the scroll!" David said excitedly. "We mustn't forget the family scroll, with the secret of the *Geula*."

"Ah, the *Geula*." Rabbi Maimon sighed. "How much longer, *Ribono Shel Olam?* We have gone through fire and water..."

His head sank into his hands. The boys looked at each other in confusion; they had never seen their father so despondent. Rabbi Maimon rubbed his eyes and got to his feet, and to their relief his voice was steady and firm. "We will have to hurry. We will leave tonight, as soon as the moon begins to wane."

"You two boys, gather together all the scrolls. I will call a meeting in the synagogue. We must try to hide the sifrei Torah... we must speak to the people and advise them what to do."

Moshe and David found sacks in the cellar. They carefully packed the scrolls, wrapping them first in cloths. When they were finished, they stood silently. Moshe could not believe that less than an hour ago they had sat securely, learning Torah in the warmth of the study. The shelves were still crowded with holy writings. What would happen to them when the house was abandoned?

"Come, David." Moshe put a hand on his younger brother's shoulder. "Let's see if we can help Batsheva."

The kitchen was fragrant with the rich, warm smell of stew. Batsheva was packing bunches of dried figs and dates into a sack. "Come along, Moshe, you strong boy. Drag this sack to the porch." Her voice was matter-of-fact and cheerful, but Moshe saw that her eyes were red-rimmed. "And you, David, run and tell your mother to pack plenty of warm clothes. Those mountains are bitterly cold, especially in the wintertime. I've heard that they are covered over with snow." She shuddered and sat down abruptly in a chair. "I don't know how I will get a wink of sleep thinking of my darlings climbing those rocky cliffs in the dark of the night."

Something was wrong. The boys looked at each other and broke out in one voice, "But, Batsheva, you are coming with us, aren't you?"

Batsheva shook her head. A single tear slipped down her plump cheek. "How can I come, children? Can you imagine fat, old Batsheva clambering over those narrow mountain trails? Why, I would be over the cliff in a moment, G-d forbid. You would have to come pick up the pieces."

The boys looked at each other uncomprehendingly. Batsheva, the one who had rocked them to sleep when they were babies and fed them honey cake when they were sad – Batsheva would be left behind?

"Batsheva, you can't stay here alone!" David's delicate face was puckered with worry. "What will happen when the Almohades come?"

"Ach – the Almohades!" Batsheva dismissed them with a toss of her head. "Who cares about them? Our Father in heaven can wipe them out with a plague, as He did the Egyptians. Or they may decide to return to Africa where they belong and leave our city alone."

"But what if they *do* come, G-d forbid?"

"Oh, then I will pour a pot of boiling oil over their heads. Or I may pretend to be a Muslim maid. I will walk like this." Batsheva picked up a clean towel, draped it over her head for a veil, and imitated the gliding walk of the Muslim women. "And they will leave me alone!"

David was smiling broadly at her antics, happily distracted, but Moshe's logical mind could not accept Batsheva's evasiveness. "But what will happen if they drive you into the town square and shout at you, 'Allah or the sword,' as they did to Father's friend? What will you do then?"

Batsheva whispered, "I don't know, Moshe. I might close my eyes tight and say *Shema Yisrael*, or... or I might take one look at those sharp swords and become a *goy*."

"Batsheva, listen to me." Moshe fought desperately to gather his thoughts, to help Batsheva understand what was ahead of her. "No one, no one on this earth can ever make you a *goy*. A Jew you were born and a Jew you will remain to the end of your life."

"And if they force me to say that Mohammed – may he have a black year – is a prophet?"

"Batsheva, do you believe it?"

"G-d forbid!" she exclaimed.

"Would you do it of your own free will?"

"Never!"

"So you are forced! And one who is forced is not held responsible. My father says that if a Jew says words out of fear of death, then those words are meaningless, and Hashem will surely forgive him. And remember, the Muslims do not ask us to deny Hashem, just to proclaim Mohammed a prophet. They do not ask us to do any deed of worship, just to say a few words."

"Ah, my little rabbi, my little *dayan*." Batsheva was now weeping in earnest. "How beautifully he speaks! Remember when you were a little boy of seven and you thought you would never become a *dayan*? Oh, what a *dayan* you will be! If only your dear mother could see you now."

"And Batsheva, remember just one more thing," Moshe added hesitantly. *How much should he say?* "Batsheva, if you do give your life for the glory of the Alm-ghty, it is the greatest thing a Jew can do. You will be taken straight to *Gan Eden*, in the garden of the holy ones, with Chana and her seven children."

"I will remember what you have told me, Moshe, my little *dayan*. I promise." Batsheva mopped her face with a clean towel. "That's enough talking now. Come, Moshe. Drag one more bag to the porch. And you, David, go tell your dear parents that supper is ready. Who knows when you will have a decent meal again?"

The night was dark with just a glimmer of moonlight when the family set out for the hills, packs strapped to their shoulders. As they headed for the country, they saw shadows detach themselves from the houses and join them silently. The procession began to climb the sandy trail, walking cautiously, mothers hushing their children. Their guide had warned them that roving bands of brigands, slave traders, and robbers were ready to ambush Jews at every turn. Silence was their best defense.

The hours passed, and all sense of excitement and adventure gave way to pain and weariness as Moshe and his brother climbed steadily upward. The sandy road grew steeper, winding treacherously among rocks and boulders. Moshe's back ached as the sack of scrolls grew heavier. "Oh, my feet!" David whispered beside him.

At last the smoky light of dawn illuminated the black peaks. It revealed a forbidding landscape, a world of slate gray rocks and gorges. Mountain after mountain unfolded against the sky. The road climbed continuously upward, boulders on one side, a sheer drop onto jagged crags on the other.

"Why, Moshe?" David whispered. "Why does Hashem make it so hard to be a Jew? Aren't we His best-loved children?"

"It is only to test us, David. Remember how Hashem tested Avraham Avinu so that He could reward him all the more in the end?"

"And when Mashiach comes," their father joined in, "all

*Moshe's back ached as the sack of scrolls grew heavier...*

the nations will see that *Am Yisrael* remained loyal and true throughout all its trials and suffering." Rabbi Maimon spoke clearly and deliberately. Moshe sensed the answer was not meant for David alone, but for all the weary people walking behind them.

"May he come speedily in our day," they murmured.

"It's getting too light to travel," the guide announced. He was a young Jew, lean and wiry, hardened from the harsh life of the mountains. "We should soon be coming to a tunnel."

Looking back, Moshe suddenly caught a glimpse of the beautiful, white silhouette of Cordova, nestled among the lush green hills. He thought of Batsheva cleaning and polishing, waiting for the Almohades. Then the road turned and seemed to dive into a series of tunnels in the rock.

"We will camp here," the guide announced.

Wearily, Moshe and David entered the cold, damp cavern. Someone lit a torch, and the tunnel stretched before them, a dark hole in the mountain. Gratefully, the boys loosened their packs. Their mother wordlessly passed out portions of bread and olives.

The murmuring voices of the mornng prayers subsided into silence as the exhausted refugees wrapped themselves in their blankets and slept.

Rabbi Maimon reached into the satchel he had been carrying and lifted out a scroll. "Come, my sons," he whispered as he opened the Gemara. "Remember what David, King of Israel, said: 'If not for Your Torah, my delight, I should have perished in my affliction.'"

Rabbi Maimon lit a candle and began to chant softly as the boys bent toward him, swaying back and forth in unison. "We were saying... *Beit Hillel* and *Beit Shammai* differ..."

# Chapter Four

# TOLEDO

"It's very different from Cordova, isn't it?" asked David. "All these gray buildings crowded together. You can hardly see the sun." Moshe nodded. It was gloomy and forbidding, this steep city of Toledo resting on a hill of granite. No wonder David was still homesick for sunny Cordova, even after the passage of time.

"But we are here, *Baruch Hashem*," Moshe reminded him. "Safe and sound and on our way to yeshiva..."

"Instead of climbing those rocky trails in the wilderness," David laughed. "You know, I still dream sometimes that I am hurtling over a cliff. And I wake up just in time."

"And to think that Rabbi Meir, Rabbi Yosef's own son, is here to teach us..." Moshe quickened his pace. "I just remembered. Rabbi Meir is going to show us two handwritten manuscripts of Rabbi Yosef's... the only two they managed to save."

They had arrived at the yeshiva, a gray stone building like all the others, but with a mezuza on the doorpost. The soft chant of learning beckoned them inside. A handful of students were already swaying over the long tables. "How wonderful to learn in a clean room instead of crouching over a flickering candle in a cave," thought Moshe.

Moshe's learning partner, Benyamin, was waiting for him. "So how is it going, Benyamin?" Moshe asked, taking out his own *sefer* and sitting down beside him.

"Terrible!" Benyamin threw up his skinny arms in despair. "*Amar Rava, Amar Abaya, shomer sachir, shomer chinam!* On the one hand and on the other hand!" His good-natured comical face bore a look of despair. "I'm lost. My father sailed through the sea of the Talmud, but I am drowning in it."

"Benyamin, it can't be that bad." Moshe put a comforting arm on his friend's shoulder. "Let's examine the problem calmly, one step at a time. What is confusing you?"

"I'll tell you why I am in trouble, Moshe", Benyamin replied seriously. "My father, may he rest in peace, built a solid foundation of learning, brick upon brick. My learning is an untidy pile of bits and pieces, a heap of odds and ends that I picked up, a little here and a little there. Maybe it's all the troubles, the wandering and hiding. Oh, I don't know. Maybe I'm just making excuses for myself and my fuzzy head."

"No, Benyamin, you're not making excuses," Moshe said earnestly. "You are right. We can't learn as we did in the olden days. All the expulsions, all the slaughters. So many yeshivot burned, so many of our teachers killed! It's not only our people who are suffering – the Torah is also suffering.

"You know, Benyamin, I have an idea." Moshe leaned forward eagerly. "I haven't told anyone about it, except my father. I would like... I would like to write an explanation of the Gemara, the first three *sedarim*. I would like to set all the different questions and discussions before the student as clearly and as briefly as possible. That way, even people who do not have the time and tranquility to study the Gemara on their own would be able to understand it. I would like, more than anything else, to help them sail through the ocean of the Talmud, as you call it, instead of floundering in it."

"You can do it, Moshe, you can do it!" Benyamin jumped to his feet excitedly and began pacing up and down the room. "You have a wonderful talent for unraveling every difficulty, for putting ideas in order. When you explain something, I understand it. And what's even better, I remember it!" Some of the students had picked up their heads and were watching Benyamin in amusement. He lowered his voice. "Write it quickly, Moshe! I will be the first to read it! And I will tell everyone that I used to learn with the great Rabbi Moshe when he was just fourteen years old and already a genius."

Moshe felt his face turning red from Benyamin's enthusiasm. To his relief, Rabbi Meir entered at that moment, and everyone in the room jumped to his feet. Rabbi Meir walked down the long room, nodding at the students as he passed. How like his holy father he looked, thought Moshe: the finely chiseled features, the deep, kind eyes. And under his arm – yes, there could be no doubt – was a packet of parchment. He had not forgotten the writing of Rabbi Yosef Ibn Migash. Rabbi Meir passed by, and Moshe was able to glimpse the companion who limped beside him. He was a stranger, a slight, stooped Jew with a graying beard. Intuitively, Moshe knew the man was a refugee. He had learned to recognize the signs – the oversized caftan, obviously borrowed, the slow, painful walk of one who had traveled over the cruel mountains on foot. But most telling of all was the look in the eyes, the look of a man who had seen his world destroyed in front of him.

A circle formed instantly around the stranger, and people questioned him anxiously. "Have you heard from Granada? Have you met any refugees from Seville?"

Moshe joined the circle. "Have you heard from... Cordova?" he asked hesitantly.

The man sighed. "You are from Cordova, my son?"

At Moshe's nod, he continued wearily. "We hid out there for a few weeks in an abandoned hut in an orchard. Some of the *Anusim* brought us food and clothing. It's all gone, destroyed. The shul, the yeshiva, nothing is left. Charred soil. A pile of rubble."

"And the people?" Moshe's voice did not sound familiar to him. "What happened to the people?"

"The people," the man repeated. "The same thing that happens to the people everywhere. Those who left their homes, well, you know yourself, son. The fortunate few survived, the others wandered over the mountains, prey to hunger, to sickness, and to bands of murderers."

"And those who remained behind?" asked Moshe.

"Those who remained behind were given a choice." The man's voice was bitter now. "They could die *Al Kiddush Hashem*, or they could pronounce a few words, and with that lie buy their lives."

"And you call that life?" a prosperous merchant spoke up. "A life of lies and fear and loneliness. A man wears the mask of a Muslim in the street and is able to be a Jew only in the solitude of his home! I would rather flee over the mountains!"

The refugee nodded. "You speak the truth," he said, "but with a naked sword suspended over our heads, how many would have the strength to refuse?"

Slowly the students dispersed, but Moshe lingered on. "Sir, perhaps you can tell me. When you were in Cordova, did you happen to hear of a woman called Batsheva?"

"Strange that you should ask me!" the refugee answered, looking at Moshe in surprise. "Several people mentioned her! It seems she was an extraordinary woman. She was a maid, I think, in the home of a rabbi, a simple, unlearned maid, and yet she showed exceptional courage and resolution. She died with *Shema Yisrael* on her lips, after calling the Almohades a bunch of murderers. She encouraged the others around her, I was told, assuring them that a special place is reserved in Gan Eden for those who die *Al Kiddush Hashem*. Why, son? Was she a relative of yours?"

Moshe leaned his face against the cool stone of the walls. "No," he whispered. "Not a relative."

*"She died with Shema Yisrael on her lips..."*

"Bad news from home?" Benyamin asked sympathetically as Moshe returned to his seat.

Moshe nodded, unable to speak. He tried to find his place in the Gemara, but the words blurred together. He saw Batsheva's kind, troubled face, her eyes red from crying, promising that she would remember what he had told her. Suddenly, Moshe seemed to hear his father's voice. "The waters overwhelm us, but the cord of Torah and mitzvot is suspended from heaven to earth. Whoever takes hold of it has hope."

Squaring his shoulders, Moshe bent over the *sefer*. "If a man gives an article to a *shomer chinam...*" With a great effort, he steadied his voice. Today's lesson was for Batsheva, he promised silently, for her merit alone. Then he remembered that she needed nothing. Her soul was shining like a star among the righteous who gave their lives to sanctify G-d's name.

All at once, the chanting of the yeshiva students was drowned out by a loud commotion in the street below. It was the roar of a crowd. Moshe heard the words, "Revenge, revenge!" Of one accord, the students streamed to the open door. Bitter experience had taught them that when there was trouble, it was often meant trouble for the Jews.

David, who had been learning with a younger group, found his brother and gripped his hand nervously. They saw that the narrow, cobbled street was thronged with Muslims in green turbans, gesturing and shouting, "Revenge, revenge!" until one voice, high and furious, shouted, "Death to the Jews!" The others took up the chant: "Revenge, revenge! Death to the Jews!"

Rabbi Meir strode into the center of the street and halted squarely in front of the mob. "What is the meaning of this?" he demanded in a steady voice. "I am the rabbi here."

"This infidel dog stole our holy treasures!" roared a Muslim.

At that moment, Moshe noticed the Jew. He was tottering between two burly Muslims, a thin wisp of a man, still wrapped in his *tallit*, his face frozen in a mask of terror.

"So where are they?" demanded Rabbi Meir. "If he stole the treasures, where has he put them?"

For a moment the noise subsided, and there was a confused buzzing. Then the high, angry voice shouted again, "Don't ask questions! Out of our way, Jew, or you will burn with him." The maddened Muslims hurtled forward, throwing Rabbi Meir against the wall as they passed. Down the narrow street rushed the angry mob, the slight figure of the Jew swept along in its wake. Cries of, "Thief, infidel, burn the lying dog!" filled the air long after they had all disappeared from view.

Pale and shaken, Rabbi Meir gathered his students inside the building and gestured at the doors, which were quickly barred. "We must find out what is happening," he said with a frown. "We must find out how it started."

"My father has a shop down the street," one of the students volunteered. "I'm sure one of his workers can tell us what is going on."

Minutes later, the frightened Jewish shopkeeper was hustled into the yeshiva room. "I have pieced together the whole story," he began agitatedly, wiping his brow with a handkerchief. "It's a lie, of course, a shameless plot. You know the mosque in the center of the city?   It contained priceless treasures of gold and precious stones. Last night the guard fell asleep, and a band of Almohades stole everything. The guard awoke and saw what had happened. He was terrified, of course, and knew he was as good as hanged for failing to guard the treasures. At that moment, poor Reb Avraham Delakfe walked by on the way to shul. The guard grabbed the Jew and started to yell, 'Thief, thief, Jewish thief!' and gathered a mob around him.  Poor Reb Avraham tried to break away and run, and that was considered proof of his guilt."

"And they believe this story?" Rabbi Meir asked.

"They believe anything, as long as it is about a Jew," the merchant retorted bitterly. "They were just waiting for an excuse to attack us, Rebbe. They have not yet forgiven Alfonso for letting the Jewish refugees settle here."

"What can we do?" one of the students asked in despair.

Moshe heard a loud banging on the door. "We are Jews, let us in," came the shout. A group of white-faced men burst in.

"They are marching through the Jewish Quarter, burning and looting."

"What's going to become of us?"

"You know what is coming," Rabbi Meir spoke heavily. "Next will come forced conversions and systematic slaughter. This is what our enemies have been waiting for." He looked at the crowd, at all the pale, frightened faces, his deep eyes full of compassion. His glance rested on David, who was clinging tightly to Moshe's hand. "My brothers, we must all return home as swiftly and as quietly as possible, take our belongings, and leave this city. Toledo is no longer a refuge for our people."

The boys hurried through the darkened streets, deliberately clinging to the black shadows of the stone buildings. We must hurry and warn Father and Mother, whispered David. "I wonder if they already know?"

It was then that Moshe remembered something. "You know, David, I never got to see the writings of Rabbi Yosef. Rabbi Meir was going to show them to me. I hope he can save them again this time."

David looked at his brother in astonishment. "Moshe, how can you worry about a piece of parchment now when we are all in danger?"

"But don't you see, David, it's all we have," cried Moshe. "It's all the Jewish people have in this bitter *Galut* – the Torah of Hashem. It's our tree of life, and we must hold on tightly to it!"

## Chapter Five

# LETTERS OF COMFORT

Rabbi Maimon sat at the head of the table and watched his daughter Miriam quietly supervise the servants as they brought in the evening meal. She was a slight, graceful girl, the youngest of his children, but there was nothing fragile about her.

Rabbi Maimon had grown up in a quieter, more peaceful world, where wives and daughters were cherished and protected. His daughter's courage and resourcefulness had never ceased to astonish him. He had seen her make a bed out of dry leaves and twigs in the wilderness and light a fire to drive away the wolves with the same quiet competence with which she now arranged the fruit in the center of the fine table in Fez. Her love for her father and brothers recognized no obstacles, allowed no room for despair.

His children had not had easy lives. Since their earliest youth, they had not known what it was to have a home. It was only now, for the first time in years, that they had found an uneasy refuge here in Morocco. They had lived the life of nomads, fleeing from town to town, from land to land, before the sword of the Almohades. It was a life of constant peril that overshadowed every happy moment. Early in their wanderings, his second wife had died, so they had been deprived of her company as well, deprived of the strong anchor of a mother's love, which nothing on earth could replace.

And yet, somehow, perhaps in the merit of their great ancestors, through the mercy of G-d, the children had grown up straight and true. The three of them, Moshe, David, and Miriam, had become all he could have wished them to be.

His eyes rested affectionately on his two sons, now deeply absorbed in conversation. The love of the boys for each other was rare and deep, totally free from the rivalry common among brothers. He called them his Yissachar and Zevulun, because, like the two sons of Jacob, they had formed a partnership. David, barely twenty-one, had become a successful diamond trader, shouldering alone the support of the family. Moshe's time, he insisted, was far too precious to waste on earning a livelihood. He must be free to devote every moment to learning and writing.

Rabbi Maimon regarded Moshe, now a serious young man of twenty-three, with a sort of wondering pride. The little boy who had been unable to learn had grown into greatness. The daring and clarity of his mind, the power of his vision, the fire of his dedication, never ceased to amaze his father.

"But there is something else," David had once said, his face glowing with brotherly pride. "It's all that, and something else. You know how most students our age are absorbed in their own growth, their own advancement? Moshe already thinks like a leader. He is always asking, 'What do our people need? How can I help them, strengthen them?'"

David must have felt his father's eyes upon him. "Father," he said, "Moshe has something to show you, something new he wrote."

Moshe was always writing. He had already completed commentaries on three sections of the Talmud, a book on logic, and an explanation of the Jewish calendar. Rabbi Maimon knew that he was now embarked on a new project, more ambitious than any he had undertaken before.

"The explanation of the Mishna?" Rabbi Maimon ventured. "I would be delighted to see it."

Moshe shook his head. His dark eyes were troubled.

"He is afraid, Father," David explained with brotherly concern.

"Afraid of what?" asked Rabbi Maimon, his eyes twinkling. "Of me?"

"No, Father. He is afraid that he made a mistake, that he might have forgotten something."

"That is impossible," declared Miriam in her positive way as she placed bread on a platter. "Moshe has never forgotten anything he has learned in his entire life. And he doesn't know how to make a mistake."

"Oh, don't say that, Miriam." Moshe's high forehead was creased with worry. "You know the way I have been writing – always on the road, always in flight, in caves, on trails, aboard ships. Half the time I didn't even have my sefarim with me."

"Moshe, Moshe, you don't need to look at sefarim," David said, only half in jest. "The Mishna and Gemara are engraved on the walls of your heart."

Moshe shook off their praise impatiently. "Please stop it, both of you. How do I know that I didn't leave something out, that I wasn't concentrating properly?"

"Concentrating!" Miriam exclaimed. "Moshe, how can you worry about concentrating? Do you remember, Father, when we ran into a squall on the way to Fez, and we were afraid that Moshe had been washed overboard, G-d forbid? Do you remember, we searched for him, everywhere..."

"And found him sitting quietly inside a coil of rope on the heaving deck," finished David, "calmly scribbling away."

"I am afraid Moshe is not in a joking mood," Rabbi Maimon admonished them. "Tell me, my son," he asked Moshe, "why are you so worried?"

"Haven't you taught us, Father, what a terrible responsibility it is to speak words of Torah to the Jewish people, especially when it concerns *halacha* and the mitzvot they must do? And the responsibility of writing it down, perhaps for posterity – is that not a hundredfold?"

"You are right, my son," Rabbi Maimon replied tranquilly. "But remember one thing, a wise man is not afraid to say, 'I've made a mistake.' If you do find one day, that in spite of all your care, you erred, all you can do is to admit it and correct it."

Moshe nodded slowly. "I will remember that. A wide, sweet smile lit up his grave face. "But please, Father, read it carefully. Search my work as an enemy, without mercy."

"As an enemy?" laughed David. "Haven't we got enough of them already?"

"As a diamond merchant, then," retorted Moshe. "Search each word for a flaw."

They were reciting the *Birchat Hamazon* when the Muslim servant entered and waited respectfully until they had finished. "A young man is here to see you," he announced. "He says he wants to see all the rabbis in this house."

Rabbi Maimon rose immediately, followed by the two boys. One never knew, in these terrible times, when a disaster might strike, G-d forbid. Ever since their arrival in Morocco, the Maimon family had been faced with a constant stream of appeals for help, advice, and guidance. To their sorrow, they had found that the terror and hostility, the forced conversions, the persecutions, had reached Morocco as well. Only because they were visitors, and because of the esteem in which they were held by the Moroccan philosophers, were the Maimons permitted to practice their faith.

Their visitor was very young, hardly more than a boy, richly dressed in the brocaded blouse of the prosperous Berbers. A wide sash of creased green silk encircled his thin waist. The face beneath the matching green turban was tense and expressionless.

"My name is Ahmed, Avraham in Hebrew. I came with my father last time on business," he began, not looking at anyone in particular. "My father doesn't know I'm here this time. I came alone. We just had a terrible fight. I guess that doesn't happen in rabbis' families." For the first time he looked directly at the elderly rabbi and added, "Fights, I mean."

"I can't really say that," Rabbi Maimon responded with a twinkle in his eye. "There are misunderstandings in every family. Ask my son, Moshe. He left home when he was quite young."

"You did?" The boy regarded the young scholar with undisguised curiosity. "You left home? Why?"

"I didn't realize," Moshe replied, "that when a father reprimands his son, it is out of love rather than anger."

"I know my father loves me," the boy said in his abrupt, choppy way. "But I can't do what he wants. I can't live his life, the life he chose for us. I have had enough of lies! I would rather die!" His voice rose. "I would rather die than live this double life. Let me be a Jew or a Berber. I cannot be both!"

"You are one of the *Anusim*, my son." The words were a statement rather than a question.

"Yes, we are the *Anusim*, the liars, the ones who stand and move our lips in their mosques, pretending to believe. They know. They glance at us out of the corners of their eyes. They sneer at our cowardice, at our disgrace. I know. I have Muslim friends. "And at home," he continued, "at home, we draw the shades. We do our mitzvot quickly, furtively, like someone hiding a shameful deed. And my father wants me to rejoice that I was born a Jew!"

"Do you know, Avraham, why your father chose this life for you? Has he ever told you?" Rabbi Maimon's gentle voice seemed to have a calming effect on the boy.

"Of course I know. He did it for us, for my brothers and me. We were babies. He could not bear to see us slaughtered before his eyes, before my mother's eyes. And he thought that he would raise us as Jews, that this would be his victory over them. They would not succeed in wiping our faith off the face of the earth." The boy paused. "That's what he thought. But it hasn't turned out that way."

"Why not?" asked Rabbi Maimon.

"Because my brothers and I started to think as we grew older, to ask questions. We have started to wonder." The boy dropped his eyes and slowly traced a pattern on the woven mat on the table before him. "We started to wonder if... if it's all worthwhile!"

"What do you mean, Avraham?"

The boy looked into Rabbi Maimon's face, and seeing no censure there, but only boundless compassion, continued. "Maybe the Almohades are right. Maybe it's true that G-d has deserted us, and chosen them to take our place." The words came out in a defiant rush. "Look at them, just look at them." The boy leaped to his feet, and pushed open the window. The loud babble of the marketplace, the shouts of vendors, the braying of donkeys came pouring into the room. "Look at their power and riches. Nation after nation has fallen before them. Look at their mosques, their palaces. And we, the Jews, are helpless and powerless. They spit at us, treat us like dirt, like the dust of the earth!"

Moshe spoke for the first time. "It is a strange thing, this dust. All living things tread on it, yet it outlasts them. And in the end, it is the dust that rises above them and covers them forever."

"Oh, you mean..." The boy smiled for the first time. "That's what my father says, that the Jewish people will outlast its enemies and triumph in the end."

But his eyes were still troubled. "But wasn't the thing that set us apart, that made us G-d's own nation, wasn't it our belief in one G-d? Well, the Almohades believe in one G-d too. They are willing to kill and be killed for their belief. Perhaps they are right. Perhaps G-d has abandoned us and has replaced our religion with theirs?"

"Listen, Avraham, listen to the promise G-d gave us in His holy Torah." Moshe fixed his earnest dark eyes on the youth. "He has promised us that He will never abandon us, never exchange us for another nation. Though we are in exile, persecuted and oppressed, we remain eternally His nation. Just think, Avraham, has G-d ever shown the miracles to other nations that He has shown to us? Has he appeared to them on Mount Sinai in fire and thunder and taught them wisdom and understanding? Appeared to a whole nation at once, to men, women, and children? As long as this has not happened, they cannot claim that they have taken our place."

The boy nodded slowly.

"So let nobody fool you, Avraham. Do not allow a counterfeit, a shallow imitation, to take the place of our true and ancient faith."

"I see... but I'm afraid..." His eyes wandered to the window again. "I'm afraid I will go home and see my Muslim friends, all of them free as the wind, and our family living in fear."

"My son, do you pray?"

Rabbi Maimon's question took the boy by surprise. "Pray? You mean, every day – *Shacharit, Mincha, Maariv?*" The boy dropped his eyes. "I'm afraid I don't. I used to, for a while, after I became a bar mitzva. My father gave me my grandfather's *tefillin*..."

"And now?" persisted the old rav.

"Now? Now I hardly do, except for Shabbat and Yom Tov. It's so hard. We have to lock up the store and go into the back room..."

"My son, you must pray every day." Rav Maimon gazed intently at the boy. "It is the thread that binds us to our Father in heaven. Our souls need it, as we need air to breathe. You must try and daven the *Shema*, even if it is only a few words, in the holy tongue. Say those words, my son. Declare that you are a child of the Jewish people. Surely..." Rabbi Maimon's voice broke, and he was silent for a while. "Surely our Merciful Father will accept the prayers of His oppressed children."

The boy regarded the older man in wonder. It amazed him that this majestic, elderly rabbi should be crying, and all because of him! "Don't worry, Rabbi. I promise to say it every day. Don't worry about me." He rose in confusion. "I will be a Jew, you will see. I will not forget. At least now I know that we are not alone. Thank you." He cast a quick glance at Moshe. "Thank you!"

He left as abruptly as he had come. For a moment the three regarded each other in silence. At last David spoke. "And there are thousands like him, all over Morocco. I meet them every day."

"And many are already lost to our people," Moshe sighed.

"I have received a letter, just today, from one of them. We must do something." Rabbi Maimon straightened with sudden determination. "We must help them. We must comfort them." He picked up his quill and dipped it into the inkstand before him. Taking a fresh parchment from the pile, he began to write as he read out loud, "Our brothers, *B'nei Yisrael*, in their suffering, may G-d quickly have mercy upon you..."[1]

"We must strengthen their faith," murmured David.

"We must answer all the doubts that were raised by this boy," added Moshe.

"And both of you must distribute these letters to the

---

[1] Iggeret Nechama, Rabbi Maimon 1160.

*Anusim* here in Morocco, and in other lands of persecution." Their father spoke with an authority that could not be questioned. "We must give them hope. They must know that they are not alone."

## Chapter Six

# TO BE A DOCTOR

David pushed open the heavy cedar door of their home, happy to escape the heat of the morning. In the cool, shadowy hallway, he nearly collided with a shabby figure dressed in a long, ragged shirt and frayed gray turban. Something about the figure looked familiar.

"Moshe!" David exclaimed.

The ragged figure turned back from the door. His brother's bright eyes peered out from a face smeared with soot. "Moshe, what on earth are you doing? Where are you..."

Moshe put a warning finger to his lips and drew David into an alcove of the entrance hall. He looked abashed, like a boy caught in mischief. "Sorry if I startled you. I'll explain everything, only please be quiet. But first of all, tell me, will I pass?"

"Pass as what?" marveled David.

"As a poor, half-witted Muslim beggar who has lost his power of speech."

"Let me see..." David looked him up and down. "Pull down your turban a bit, those sharp eyes give you away. Otherwise not bad. Now tell me what you are up to."

"I am going to apply for a job as janitor for a physician."

"A janitor?" David regarded his brother with growing concern. "Moshe, are you sure you are feeling quite well?"

"Thank G-d, I'm quite well and have not taken leave of my senses. David, I have decided to take up the study of medicine. Now, don't protest," Moshe added, raising a restraining hand. "You have supported our family long enough. The time has come to do my share. And what could be a better profession than helping to alleviate suffering, perhaps even to save lives? So why the disguise? Listen. The best physician here in Fez is also a bitter enemy of our people. On three different occasions I have asked him to allow me to study under him, and each time he refused. The last time I applied, he ordered the servant to throw me out. So you see..." Moshe spread his hands expressively.

"So you are going to become an unofficial member of his school. David tried hard to repress a smile."

"Exactly. While I'm busy wielding my broom and my scrubbing brush, I can listen and learn. And he certainly will not suspect a poor half-wit, who is mute as well, of being a Jewish student in disguise."

"And if he recognizes you while you are playing this trick on him, do you know what your life will be worth?" David asked seriously.

"Don't worry, David. A good servant becomes invisible after a while. With G-d's help, I will be perfectly safe. There is one thing that is bothering me, of course." Moshe frowned. "Is one permitted to deceive a fellow man? But in this case, I feel it is permissible. This physician is totally unscrupulous. He treats only the rich, who can afford to pay his fees, and drives the poor out of his house with blows and curses. He serves himself, not humanity. And of course, he will never admit a Jewish patient." With a grin Moshe adjusted his turban and tightened his ragged belt. "I must go now before he leaves for his midday rest. And don't say anything to Father. It would only worry him."

David looked after his brother doubtfully. Then a smile broke across his face; he reminded himself that Moshe had never yet failed at anything he had undertaken. He watched from the doorway as Moshe's ill-clad form retreated into the distance and prayed that Hashem would watch over him.

Moshe walked briskly along the narrow, twisting streets of Fez. On both sides rose the steep, towering walls of the Moorish neighborhood. There was no telling, Moshe mused, what secret lives went on behind these locked and barred facades. One might hide the luxurious home of a Moorish nobleman, the walls hung with costly tapestries, the benches piled with silk cushions. In another home, a secret Jew might be winding his *tefillin* around his arm with a whispered prayer, while his wife watched from a corner, reciting *Tehillim*.

At last he arrived at the house he was seeking. Moshe knocked vigorously on the door. A servant thrust his head through the doorway and looked suspiciously at him. Moshe made quick motions of scrubbing and sweeping. The servant opened the door wider and allowed him to enter the long, whitewashed hallway. The smell of herbs and medication assailed his nostrils. "You want work?" the servant said shortly. "Wait here. I'll ask my master."

At that moment the door to the doctor's study opened, and Moshe heard a harsh voice. "Get out and don't ever come back!" A young woman came hurrying out, holding a wailing baby. The tall, corpulent figure of the physician appeared in the doorway. "For free, you want me to treat you? If I treat you, then why not all the rabble in Fez? Don't come here again, because I will have you thrown out." He brandished a scalpel at her as she fled through the doors and then turned a furious, flushed face toward Moshe and the servant. "What? Another beggar who wants medication? Throw him out before..."

"No, master," the servant said hurriedly. "This one is looking for work, to help with the cleaning. The master has said we need someone for the operating room."

The physician glanced at the beggar indifferently. "Can you scrub and sweep?"

Moshe nodded vigorously.

"He can't speak, my master," the servant explained.

"All the better. He will mind his own business! Put him to work and see what he can do."

Eagerly, Moshe grabbed a broom and began sweeping the inner room. When he had finished, he found a pail and brush and began scrubbing the operating table and the cupboards.

*"Get out and don't ever come back!"*

All day Moshe worked and listened. The fat man was a capable physician. Moshe watched him examine each patient quickly, sometimes pinpointing the malady simply by looking into the sick man's face. His first question to every patient, even those brought in on stretchers by anxious relatives, was, "Can you pay?" Then he stated the cost of the treatment. If the patient or his relatives hesitated, they were thrown out with curses.

Moshe bent his head over his work to hide his distress. When he became a physician, he would treat rich and poor, friend and foe exactly alike. Were they not all human beings, created in Hashem's image?

In the middle of the afternoon, a group of richly-clad Muslims came hurrying in, carrying a stretcher on which a very ill man lay groaning and twitching in pain.

"My father is suffering terrible agonies – a tremendous pain in his head," one of the young men cried urgently to the doctor. "It is so bad that at times he loses consciousness."

"We shall see." The doctor began to examine the patient carefully, lifting his eyelids, exploring the skull with his fingers. At last he proclaimed in a pompous manner, "Your father is suffering from a parasite. It is a worm, I believe, eating away inside his brain. It must be removed immediately."

The family nodded anxiously and filed out into the waiting room.

The physician's helpers, two Muslim students, administered a sleeping potion to the groaning patient. Within moments, the doctor expertly slit open the man's skull and examined his brain. "Look, there it is! Do you see?" He pointed inside the open skull.

The students crowded around him. "Yes," they exclaimed excitedly, "just as the professor said. Right in the center of the brain!" The physician took a sharp needle and began probing at the gray mass inside the skull. The room was silent, except for the labored breathing of the patient.

"I can't get it out," the physician growled anxiously. "He can't last much longer. You, there," he called to one of the students. "Feel his pulse!"

Moshe could restrain himself no longer. He walked over to the operating table. "You need a green leaf," he said. All eyes turned to him.

"What!" The physician let out an incredulous roar. "You're supposed to be mute! And what nonsense are you talking? Can't you see that a life is at stake?"

"That is exactly why I am speaking to you. You must get a green leaf immediately. It will save this man's life!"

The physician regarded him for a moment in silence. "All right," he barked suddenly. "What can we lose? You – run to the patio and bring some leaves."

Swiftly, Moshe grabbed the plant and detached a leaf from the bunch. He held it toward the spot where the soft tissue of the brain was exposed. The surface trembled, and a fat worm crawled slowly onto the leaf. "Thank G-d," exclaimed Moshe as he dropped the leaf into a jar.

The physician bent over the incision and and quickly sewed it shut. He felt the pulse of the patient. "He will live – thanks to you," he said, examining Moshe with his piercing, black eyes. "I believe I know you. You are no Muslim beggar! You are Moshe, the son of Maimon, the Jewish philosopher."

Moshe nodded.

"I understand why you deceived me. You could have fooled me forever. It was a wonderful way to learn my secrets. But tell me, why did you give yourself away?" the physician regarded him with intense curiosity.

"How could I be silent?" Moshe exclaimed. "A human life was at stake."

"And do you think I will allow you to stay here now – now that you have admitted your origins?"

Moshe shook his head. "I don't suppose so. I am sorry, because there is much I could have learned from you." He picked up the broom he had dropped, put it back in its place, and turned to the door.

The physician's voice called him back, and in it could be heard a grudging note of respect. "Stop. There is much I can learn from you as well. You may stay on as my student. There are many doctors, but only a few who are born healers. You may be one of the few."

Moshe hurried through the winding streets, his steps light as air. The events of the afternoon flashed before his eyes, and he saw clearly that it was Divine Providence that had guided him to the doctor's house and had won him the arrogant man's trust and respect. Medicine would be one more way in which he could serve his Creator and help his suffering brothers. Was it not written, 'In all your ways shall you know Him?'

As he turned a corner, he saw the dying rays of the sun painting the sky crimson and lavender. He would have to hurry to wash up and change from his rags in order to catch the *Mincha* service in his father's study. He smiled as he thought of how much David would enjoy his account of the day's adventure.

As soon as he entered the study, Moshe sensed that something was wrong. The service had not yet begun. Rabbi Maimon sat slumped in his seat with one hand over his eyes.

Avraham stood in front of him, his face white as chalk, his voice anguished. "Rabbi Maimon, what do you say? Have you an answer? Can you answer me?"

Rabbi Maimon was silent.

"Then it is all over for us," Avraham said dully. "All the struggle. All the fear. It was all in vain. We aren't Jews anyway."

Moshe regarded Avraham in alarm. Over the past two years this troubled young son of the *Anusim* had grown into a devoted scholar of the Torah. He managed to slip away almost every night to study with Rabbi Maimon and his sons, shrugging off their concern for his safety. His excitement and eagerness reminded Moshe of his own first year in yeshiva, when the gates of wisdom had opened before him. What could possibly have caused his wild and bitter words?

"Avraham, will you please tell me what you are talking about?" Moshe asked calmly.

Avraham spun around to face him. He thrust a sheet of parchment into Moshe's hand, as though it burned to the touch. "Here, here is what I'm talking about. Read this, and you will know. We are traitors, outcasts. Cut off from the community of Israel. We have stood in the mosques of the Muslims. We have worshipped idols just by standing there. Our prayers are hateful to Hashem, our mitzvot are abominations. Go ahead, read. See for yourself." Angrily, he brushed a sleeve across his eyes.

Moshe scanned the letter rapidly. It had been written by a rabbi living in the lands that had not suffered religious persecution. The rabbi was answering the question of one of the Anusim from Morocco: "When a Jew is given the choice of acknowledging Mohammed or being put to death, what should he do?" The answer of the rabbi was harsh and unbending. Every Jew must allow himself to be killed rather than accept the religion of Mohammed. Failing to do so, he would be forever cut off from the Jewish people. The Anusim, he ruled, were idol worshippers in every way and were to be treated accordingly.

Moshe read the answer. He looked from his father to Avraham with growing comprehension. His father was watching many years of patient labor, during which he had struggled to strengthen the communities of Morocco, being destroyed by a few reckless words. And Avraham – Avraham who had clung to the Rock of Israel with his last powers of faith and courage – was being hurtled over the abyss.

"Father," Moshe said softly.

Rabbi Maimon lifted his eyes. "Moshe, my son. I have no strength. Answer. Your turn has come."

Moshe took a deep breath. "Avraham, listen to me. The author of this letter is making a terrible mistake. He has misunderstood the law of the Torah. After *Mincha*, I will explain it all to you."

"You mean..." Avraham's eyes searched Moshe's. "I should still pray? Are you sure I'm allowed to...?"

Moshe placed a *siddur* in his hand and intoned, "*Ashrei yoshvei veitecha...*"

Everyone was much calmer after *Mincha*. "Now let us examine this letter and see what merit it has," Moshe began. "It seems to me that the rabbi has written this letter without careful consideration, without understanding of the Jewish Law, and without compassion for a Jewish soul. He has had no experience of what we have undergone. Do you remember what we learned in *Pirkei Avot*? 'Do not judge your friend until you have been in his place.'"

"But isn't he supposed to be a learned man, a great scholar?" asked Avraham. "Though I am sure he is no match for

Rabbi Maimon and yourself." The color had returned to Avraham's face, and he looked almost his old self again.

"The rabbi has not read carefully, and has misunderstood what he read. He calls you idol worshippers and doesn't stop to think that the *Anusim* did not choose to serve idols for gain or pleasure. They were forced into it, by fear of death.

"He rules that every Jew must give his life rather than convert. He has not troubled to examine our situation and to see that the Mohammedans do not demand that we worship idols or perform any action or religious ritual. All they ask is that we acknowledge the prophet Mohammed. And our enemies themselves know that we do not mean it, that we will continue to serve G-d in our homes."

"Yes, it is a great mitzva to sanctify G-d's name, to die *Al Kiddush Hashem*," Moshe continued. For a second he saw before him the face of an old woman, left behind in Cordova. She had promised to be brave, and she had kept her promise as she faced the swords of the murderers. "But if a Jew is unable to do so, to make the supreme sacrifice, that does not make him a worshipper of idols. And to say that Hashem will punish one for the mitzvot he performs, for the *tefillot* he recites..." Moshe rose, unable to contain his anger any longer. "Our just G-d does not hold back the reward of any creature, even the most wicked. Certainly He will reward you for every mitzva that you do in the midst of your suffering, for every prayer you whisper in the lands of your enemies."

"Rabbi Moshe, son of Maimon, thank you." There were tears in Avraham's eyes. "Only such a father could have such a son! But do me one more favor. Write it all down, just as you said it to me. I must show it to my father. Since we received this terrible letter, he hasn't left the house. He won't eat, he won't even talk to us, except to say, 'We are cut off, cut off...'"

Moshe glanced questioningly at his father, who nodded. "It is your turn, Moshe. The time has come for you to step forward and speak to the entire Jewish people. May Hashem be with you!"

Moshe reached for a parchment on the desk, dipped his quill into ink, and began to write: "A man of our times turned to one of our scholars and asked him about the forced conversions in our day..."[2]

---

[2] Iggeret HaShmad, Rabbi Moshe ben Maimon (Maimar Kiddush Hashem).

# Chapter Seven

# IN HIDING

In the freshness of the early morning, Rabbi Moshe walked along the winding streets of Fez. He held the long green spear of his *lulav* aloft, taking care not to let its tip catch on the overhanging balconies. The palm of his hand cradled a golden *etrog*, blanketed in layers of flax.

The streets of the Jewish Quarter were deserted. The morning sun slanted through the narrow streets, but no Jews could be detected hurrying along, nor any palm branches waving in joyous procession. If any *sukkot* had been built, they were well concealed behind walled courtyards.

The Jews were afraid. They bided their time tensely behind locked doors and shuttered windows, waiting for the storm to pass. After years of uneasy quiet, the terror of the Almohades had been unleashed once again against the Jewish community. Just four days earlier, David had burst into his father's study and told him in a trembling voice that Rabbi Yehuda Ibn Shushan had been murdered. The great rabbi from Baghdad, revered by Muslims as well as Jews, had once enjoyed the protection of Moroccan rulers and had been free to teach and to learn. It was because of him that Rabbi Maimon had chosen Fez as their place of refuge, and they had been permitted to live openly as Jews in the lion's den itself, the birthplace of the Almohades.

But now the great light had been snuffed out. In the marketplace, a horde of Muslims with lifted swords had screamed, "Allah or the sword!" and Rabbi Yehuda had made his choice.

Rabbi Moshe sighed deeply. The words of one of the Shabbat prayers went through his mind. "Beloved and pleasant in their lives, even in death they were not parted from Him. They were swifter than eagles, stronger than lions to carry out the will of their Maker..."

Rabbi Moshe shook his head. It was *Succot*, the season of rejoicing. Mourning was forbidden. Resolutely, he lifted the proud banner of his *lulav*. Was not this very *lulav* a symbol of victory, a flag flying proudly over territory won from the enemy?

Lost in thought, Rabbi Moshe did not notice the group of riders until they were almost upon him. Muslims, richly attired in brilliant silk robes, with pearls and precious stones studding the bridles of their donkeys, bore down upon the solitary thinker. Rabbi Moshe recognized the ruler of the city at the head of the procession.

He was a short, broad man, dressed in rich clothing embroidered with gold and silver thread. The jewels in his white turban rivaled those adorning his donkey. Rabbi Moshe stood aside and waited for the group to pass, but the governor and his officers rode to the center of the street, blocking the narrow road.

"Well, now, Rabbi Moshe," came the silky voice of the governor. "I must say, I am surprised at you, surprised and disappointed. You are the brilliant philosopher, the scientist and physician, and yet you too..." He pointed to the *lulav* in Rabbi Moshe's hand and began to laugh uproariously. His officers followed suit, pointing at Rabbi Moshe and bellowing with laughter. "It's hard to believe that you could stand here and wave grass around your head, like the other fools and ignoramuses."

"You are mistaken," Rabbi Moshe replied, waves of anger rising within him. Even as he heard the cautious voice of reason counseling silence, he heard his own voice, ringing with defiance. "The *lulav* and *esrot* in my hand are not the custom of fools. It is the commandment of our eternal and holy Torah, given to us as a priceless gift."

"The custom of fools and ignoramuses," the other repeated as if he had heard nothing. "Don't you think it is time, my esteemed Rabbi Moshe ben Maimon, that you freed yourself of these idiotic superstitions?"

Rabbi Moshe's control broke. "As I said, you are mistaken. If you wish to see fools and ignoramuses, then go – go to Mecca!"

There was a collective gasp from the Muslims.

"Yes, go," he continued, "go and see them throwing stones at their holy mountains! Is there a greater idiocy than that?"

The small, fat man stiffened in his saddle. His face darkened beneath the white turban. Without another word, he turned his mount sharply and rode away, followed by his escorts.

"It was a mistake," Rabbi Moshe murmured to himself as he watched their retreating backs. The proud, cruel man would not allow the insult to his faith to pass unavenged. He should have held his tongue; it was a sin to endanger one's life needlessly. "But Master of the Universe," he murmured, "how could I have stood by and allowed Your holy commandments to be trampled in the dust?"

He pushed all worry aside as he entered the *beit k'nesset*. The long, vaulted room was almost empty. Only a few hardy souls had braved the anger of the Muslims on this troubled *Chol Hamoed* and had left their homes to attend the *minyan*. They prayed with fervor and energy, then marched around the *bima*, *lulavim* held high. "*Ana Hashem, hoshia na* – Help us, oh L-rd, save us!" Some wept.

Once back at home, Rabbi Moshe's fears returned. Taking two steps at a time, he hurried up to the apartment. David had remained at home with their father and sister. He prayed silently for their safety as he unlocked the door with trembling hands. David stood in the doorway, a finger on his lips. He closed the door softly and motioned his brother inside. "Moshe, hurry, we must leave. Muhammed warned us. The governor has ordered us all to be imprisoned."

Cold fear gripped Moshe's heart. "What about Father? And Miriam?"

"They are safe, both of them. Avraham has found us a hiding place, an attic in a deserted house on the outskirts of town.

He took them there this morning. Hurry, Moshe," he urged, handing him a canvas bag. "Pack the scrolls you need the most! The wagon is waiting in the courtyard."

Rabbi Moshe glanced at his father's desk. It was piled high with *sefarim*. Rabbi Maimon must have selected them and must then have been forced to leave them behind for lack of space. Moshe's heart twisted at the thought of the elderly rabbi being torn from his quiet study once again. After being driven from one end of the earth to the other, could he endure much more wandering and deprivation in the twilight of his years?

Bitter remorse swept over him. "It's all my fault," he said. "I should have kept quiet, for the sake of my father, for that alone."

"Don't be foolish, Moshe. They were waiting for an opportunity, for a pretext to be rid of us. They have never forgiven you for the letter you wrote about Muslim persecution. Come now, we must hurry."

With a backward glance, the brothers closed the door on the spacious apartment, on five years of peace and tranquility.

A lone Muslim stood patiently in the courtyard beside a wagon piled high with hay. With a quick motion of his hand, he gestured to the two young men to get into the back and lie down. "This is going to be prickly," he warned, as he heaped hay over them.

The wagon had just rolled out of the courtyard when a group of armed Muslims, mounted on horses, hurtled past them

*... a group of armed Muslims, mounted on horses, hurtled past them
and thundered into the yard of their house.*

and thundered into the yard of their house. They heard the crunch of timber as the men broke through the outside door. The wagon proceeded at a leisurely pace for a minute or two, then the driver whipped the donkey into a gallop.

"*Baruch Hashem*," murmured David. "G-d is with us. Had we waited another minute... They are in the house now, tearing it apart, searching for us."

It was only when the driver came to a stop that the brothers emerged from the hay. They brushed off their clothing and climbed stiffly out of the wagon. The house they entered was small and insignificant, screened from the road by a few scraggly palm trees. Carrying their sacks, they made their way up a steep, narrow flight of steps that led to the attic.

"Bend your head," David warned Moshe as they entered the low doorway. There, in the dim interior, sat Rabbi Maimon and their young sister. The father rose with outstretched arms, and the young girl gave a cry of joy. "*Baruch Hashem, Baruch Hashem.* We were so worried about you!"

Moshe and David sat down on the bare furniture and recounted their close escape. Rabbi Maimon had his Gemara open before him, and the candle cast a circle of light over the small group.

"Well, my sons, it is all for the best," he said, a smile tugging at his lips. "You boys have been running around a lot, David in search of his diamonds, Moshe after his potions and herbs. Here we'll have some peace at last. Now we can learn together, and Moshe will make some progress with his work on the Mishna..." Moshe returned his father's smile, filled with gratitude at the old scholar's indomitable faith. How could he have doubted his father's endurance?

"That's all very well, Father," their sister broke in. Her white brow was puckered with worry. "But what will we do for food? We are prisoners here. They are searching for us all over Fez. When this sack of flour is gone, and the jar of oil..."

There was a knock on the door, three soft knocks, three loud. It was Avraham, his arms loaded with bundles. His eyes swept the room, and a wide smile of relief split his tense face. "*Baruch Hashem*, you are all safe!"

"And thank you, G-d's messenger!" Rabbi Maimon replied, looking at his pupil fondly. "We could not have escaped without you."

"How true!" David added. "Without Avraham..."

With a quick gesture of his arm, Avraham brushed aside their gratitude. "And without you, without Rabbi Maimon, would I be a Jew today? Look," he said, bending down to separate the packages, "here are some barley and wheat grains, dried dates, and raisins, flatbread and water as well. I am afraid you must not leave this house, at least not for a while. It's dark and cramped, I know, but at least it is reasonably safe. Don't worry, we're working on a plan. We must get you out of this country. It's no place for a real Jew any more. Only *Anusim* like us can survive," he added with a touch of bitterness.

Rabbi Moshe met his eyes with quick sympathy. He knew how Avraham hated the double life he was forced to lead, hiding his Jewishness from the public eye, practicing the Torah in secrecy.

"But at least we can be of help to you now since we are free to come and go as we please," Avraham continued. "The only question is... where will you go now?"

"Yes, where?" repeated David. "Is there a land in the world that is safe for our people these days?"

David's question was met with silence. For a moment Rabbi Moshe saw the trail of communities lying in ruins across Spain and Africa, the proud yeshivot in ashes, men, women, and children slaughtered without mercy. But was it any better in the West? He knew that in France and in Germany Jews were being herded into ghettos, spit upon, branded with a badge of shame. Sudden weariness pressed down upon him. "It's hard to choose between the East and the West," he murmured.

Rabbi Maimon had been sitting motionless, his gray eyes staring straight ahead, unseeing. Suddenly he spoke. "You are right, my children. There is no place for a Jew in *Galut*. Let us go to *Eretz Yisrael* instead and await the coming of Mashiach there."

"*Eretz Yisrael?*" David turned to his father incredulously. "But Father, our holy land is in the very heart of the storm! The land is in ruins, the Jewish community tiny, impoverished. And the two great powers of earth are fighting over it, each trying to tear it from the other's grasp." Even as he spoke the discouraging words, there was an undercurrent of excitement in his voice.

"And our people are being crushed between them," Moshe added bitterly. "When the Crusaders entered the holy city to 'free' it from the infidels, their cruelty outdid that of our Muslim rulers. They herded the Jews of Yerushalayim into the great synagogue and burned them alive."

"May G-d avenge their blood," murmured their young sister, who sat plying her needle, her bright eyes darting from one to the other. "They slaughtered all who crossed their path. And then the blood-soaked butchers went to give thanks for a holy victory in their house of worship."

Rabbi Maimon did not seem to have heard any of this. "If only I will merit to see the Holy Land, to kiss the blessed earth of *Eretz Yisrael* before I die. Yes, yes, that is what I pray for."

Moshe opened his lips to protest, to assure his father that many fruitful years lay before him, but something in the pale translucence of his father's face trapped the words in his throat. They would have to hurry if Rabbi Maimon's dream of seeing the Holy Land could ever be fulfilled.

## Chapter Eight

# STORM AT SEA

*Eretz Yisrael!* From that moment on, they had hardly ceased to speak of it. Day after day, week after week, as the cramped walls of the attic seemed to close in on them, they discussed their dream. The obstacles were overwhelming. Other Jews, driven by longing that defied reason, had braved the journey. In letters home, the survivors had told their tales of the difficult trek across the Mediterranean landscape, of the burning deserts where the horses sank knee-deep into the sand. They wrote of highwaymen, swift as leopards, who crouched behind stones on the wayside and hurled bamboo lances tipped with iron at the travelers.

They had written of the desert littered with heaps of camel bones and the abandoned possessions of those who had died there. They warned of the brackish water that could cause a traveler to sicken and die, of the winds that blew from the four corners of the world, choking the throat with dust. They wrote of the Muslim guides who would lure a traveler into a desolate spot to murder him and rob him of his belongings.

Yet, even as Rabbi Maimon's family reasoned and weighed the risks, their longing grew until it was a fire raging inside of them. To walk where Avraham Avinu had walked, to stand where the prophets had stood, to pray at the grave of Rochel Imeinu, to embrace the stones of the Kotel Hamaaravi – these were all-encompassing desires.

And suddenly, they were not speaking of "if" but "how." Their discussions centered on the best time to make the journey, from which port to set sail. Avraham came often to tell them that such a trip was lunacy and therefore forbidden by the Torah. Had not Rabbi Moshe taught him of the duty to guard one's life? Yet even as he shook his head in dismay, he made inquiries for them, and in his precise merchant's hand drew up long lists of provisions necessary for the journey.

On a clear night at the end of the month of *Nissan*, five figures slipped out separately from a deserted house at the edge of town. Rabbi Moshe paused to breathe in the pure night air. It was six months since he had been out of doors.

David held the reins of the horse as Avraham loaded the wagon with provisions. Moshe helped his father up the wagon step. Rabbi Maimon moved with steady dignity, but Moshe felt his father's arm trembling with age. His heart sank as he thought of the long, perilous journey over sea and desert that lay before them.

The clip-clop of the horses' hooves echoed loudly over the cobbled streets. No one followed them; still, they sat forward, tense and anxious, until the wagon was on the open dirt road winding down between the rounded hills.

All night they traveled. Slowly the red thread of dawn shot

across the horizon. They paused to wash and pray, and then drove on. The sun was over the horizon by the time they reached the seaport, the sea breeze fresh and salty in their faces.

On the dock, all was noise and confusion. Porters carried heavy caskets to the small boats which were rowed out to the ships. Passengers jostled each other in their eagerness to get on board.

Avraham helped them unload their wagon and stack the provisions in one of the small rowboats waiting at the dock. They climbed into the boat, their young sister first, her bright brown eyes sparkling above her veil, then Rabbi Maimon and his two sons. The family turned to part with Avraham, but he climbed into the boat with them.

"Avraham, you have done enough," protested Rabbi Moshe. "You don't have to accompany us to the ship."

"More than enough," agreed David. "There is a long journey before you. Start back now, and thank you for everything."

Avraham shook his head. "Have you not taught me that a pupil accompanies his master a distance of a mile, and his chief teacher, three miles? Haven't you all been my teachers, my chief teachers?" His voice broke. Wordlessly, Rabbi Moshe put his arm around the young man's thin shoulders.

The sailor pushed off and began to row toward the ship with long, practiced strokes. The ship was an old, weatherbeaten craft, its ancient deck worn smooth, its hull darkened by the gales and tempests of many days' sailing.

The burly captain, as weather-beaten as his craft, roared last-minute instructions to the riggers at the masthead. The anchor was up, the sails were set. Avraham clambered into the rowboat that would return him to shore. "Go in peace, and may Hashem watch over you," he called. He waved his scarf as the strip of water widened between them. They stood and watched him go – their friend and pupil, who had risked so much for their sake. "Students are like one's own children," murmured Rabbi Maimon. Tears brightened his gray eyes.

They turned their faces toward the open sea. The ship glided gently forward. A cool breeze sent ripples across the shiny water. Six days passed, and the ship rocked softly on the tranquil sea. Little, silvery waves lapped against the bow, white clouds floated high in the sky above them. Rabbi Maimon and his sons leaned on the railing and spoke about the Gemara they were learning together or of questions that had come up in the commentary that Rabbi Moshe was writing on the Mishna. Their sister sat on the deck close by, busy with her needlework or saying the comforting words of *Tehillim*.

On Shabbat, the seventh day at sea, the water clouded over treacherously and the wind began to rise. The sea darkened and heavy clouds covered the sky. Drops of rain became spikes of hail. Suddenly the wind seemed to come from all directions at once. Huddled below the deck, Rabbi Moshe and his family listened to the terrible noise that filled the air – the howl of the wind, the roar of the waves, the claps of thunder. Lightning came like a shower of fire. The wind hurled the ship against the sea. *The boat spun and pitched* as the sailors fought to right the mast. The ship was lifted to fearful heights, then hurled sharply to the depths. Cries of terror filled the craft and rose above the terrible roar of the water, which was now washing in from all sides.

Throughout that long and terrifying Shabbat, they rode through the storm, the boards of the ship groaning and creaking beneath them. Never for a moment did Rabbi Moshe cease his prayers. At last, in late afternoon, the wind relented. Slowly the ship righted itself and began to sail across the rough, white-capped sea. The storm was over.

"It's a miracle. G-d saved us!" The captain's craggy face had lost its perpetual scowl, and a look of wonder softened his harsh features. "Never have I met with such a storm. In another minute we would have capsized."

Rabbi Moshe nodded. *"Men who go to the sea in ships and work in great waters,"* he quoted, *"have seen the miracles of G-d.* I will never forget this day," he added to David, as they stood by the railing and contemplated the once-more tranquil sea. Their father and sister were resting below deck. The last half of the sun sank beneath the horizon, and the sea flamed under its brilliant light. "I will never forget this storm, when the sea rose against us to drown us. I have resolved, David, that the day we embarked on our journey and this day of the storm will both be fast days for me and for my children after me. No food or drink

*The boat spun and pitched...*

will pass our lips, and we will give as much *tzedaka* as we can.

"And just as on this day, I found no one – none but the Holy One, Blessed Be He... so will I see no man on those days, and speak to no one, unless I am forced to do otherwise."[3]

It was the third day of the month of *Sivan*, and they stood on the deck, straining to catch sight of land. Suddenly, through the golden haze of morning, Moshe saw a hill rising from the sea. It was noble, unsinkable, untouched by time. "Land, land," rose the cry all around them.

"*Eretz Yisrael*," whispered Rabbi Maimon.

They stood upon the parched yellow earth of Acco and bent to kiss the earth. The four of them stood still for a moment, each lost in silent prayer, thanking Hashem for His mercies. "Blessed are You, Who has granted us life, Who has sustained us and enabled us to reach this moment."

Standing under the radiant sun of *Eretz Yisrael*, the land upon which G-d's eye rests eternally, Rabbi Moshe made one more promise. "This day, the happiest day of my life," he vowed, "will be a day of joy and gladness for me and my family after me; a day to feast and rejoice and to give presents to the poor, to the end of all generations."[4]

---

[3] From the Rambam's letters in Sefer HaChareidim.
[4] Ibid

## Chapter Nine

# IN THE HOLY LAND

If a Jew lives in *Eretz Yisrael*, all his sins are forgiven."
Rabbi Moshe had chosen the theme of *Eretz Yisrael* for his lesson.
Perhaps it would awaken some interest, some hope, in the weary
group that sat around him in the little, whitewashed synagogue.
It was late afternoon, between the *Mincha* and *Maariv* services,
and the men of Eilat were worn from a day spent laboring under
the blazing sun. One was hunched forward, his gray head resting
on his arms. It was hard to tell if he was asleep or awake.

The old *shamash* of the synagogue was certainly asleep.
He sat bolt upright against the wall, snoring gently, his white
beard fanning out over his meager chest. No matter, thought
Rabbi Moshe. The Jewish people might sleep, but their hearts
were always awake.

"If a man walks even four cubits in the land of Israel, he is
assured eternal life." There was a slight stir at these words. The
gray-haired man lifted his head from his arms. He had been
awake after all. A young man nudged the sleeping *shamash*, who
stirred and blinked.

They paid dearly for the right to live in the Holy Land,
these poor Jewish workers. They eked out their meager living by
stirring great vats of corrosive dye, which had stained their arms

and legs a deep crimson. And, as if their poverty were not enough, they lived in constant fear of war and violence. Caught between the warring Crusaders and fanatic Arabs who were battling over *Eretz Yisrael*, they were at the mercy of both. Frustrated by the long, drawn out conflict, both Muslims and Christians were quick to vent their anger on the Jewish "nonbelievers" who lived unarmed in their midst.

"Our sages used to kiss the rocks, the dust on the borders of Israel, and brought their dead to be buried here in sacred ground."

He had his audience at last. The men were leaning forward attentively, stained hands resting on their knees. Even young Eliezer, the only child in the group, was listening. He was a skinny, restless boy of about twelve, who had sighed and squirmed throughout the previous lessons. His limbs were covered with open sores caused by the abrasive dyes, and he picked at his arms constantly. Rabbi Moshe had prepared an ointment for him which he hoped would help, but for the moment Eliezer seemed to have forgotten his affliction. His large, bright eyes shone straight into Rabbi Moshe's face.

"... because just by resting in the earth of the Holy Land he will receive atonement. You will remember," continued Rabbi Moshe, "that our father Yaakov begged his son Yosef to bury him in Israel."

"And so did Yosef, also Yosef," the boy's high young voice cut in eagerly. "He made his brothers promise not to leave Egypt

*Even young Eliezer, the only child in the group, was listening.*

until they had taken his coffin..." His father, a tall, black-browed man, gave him a stern look, for children did not speak before their elders; but the boy finished quickly, ". . . which was resting on the bottom of the Nile."

"Well said!" Rabbi Moshe nodded at the boy and reassured the father with a smile. He explained that while all of the land was holy, the greatest holiness, of course, rested on the city of Yerushalayim and the site of the *Beit HaMikdash*. The Divine Presence had once rested there, and it could never be banished.

"Even though the land has been wrested from us," he concluded, "even though it lies barren and abandoned, that holiness remains intact for all time, until the coming of Mashiach, swiftly in our day."

A heartfelt "Amein" rumbled from the listeners, the boy's voice ringing out among them. The room had gradually darkened during the lesson; evening had come, reducing the group to shadowy shapes in the falling dusk. The old shamash rose and shuffled to the *bima* to light two candles. The congregation stood and swayed over their prayers, the straight light of the flames casting huge shadows onto the plastered walls.

After *Maariv* the men slowly dispersed, nodding respectfully at Rabbi Moshe as they filed out. The murmur of their weary voices floated back through the night.

"Eliezer," Rabbi Moshe called, "I have something for you. Ask your father if you can come with me for a few moments."

The boy was gone in a burst of flying legs and returned

moments later. "I can come."

They walked together under the glowing stars toward Rabbi Moshe's home at the bottom of the hill. They had rented a house close to the *beit k'nesset* upon their arrival from Morocco, for the aged Rabbi Maimon could no longer walk far on Shabbat and holy days.

In his brightly lit study, Rabbi Moshe showed Eliezer the small jar of ointment. "This will heal your sores and relieve the pain."

"Medicine?" The boy backed away, his eyes wide with fright. "No, I don't need anything. I always have them. It's nothing."

"Come, Eliezer, you will see it doesn't hurt at all." Gently he spread the mixture over the boy's rigid arms and legs. At last Eliezer relaxed, and a wide smile spread across his slender face. "It doesn't hurt at all. It feels good. I didn't know you fixed up bodies and not just souls."

"The two depend on each other," answered Rabbi Moshe.

"Rabbi Moshe," the boy began as he watched the rabbi scrub his hands. "Have you ever been to Yerushalayim?"

"Not yet – but I will go very soon," Rabbi Moshe replied, explaining that in a few days Rabbi Yafet, the Rav of Acco, would be accompanying him and his whole family on a trip to see the holy city.

"You mean, you are going to see the *Har HaBayit*, the

place where the Divine Presence is resting?"

Rabbi Moshe nodded, "Yes, my son, and with G-d's help, we will go to Chevron, too – to see the cave where our fathers Avraham, Yitzchok, and Yaakov lie buried."

"Oh, please, please, can I go with you?" The words broke out in a desperate cry. "I have never been there! And I will help you. I will water the donkeys. I'm good at loading, and my sores will heal better if I don't mix the dye. My father will allow me to go, I know he will."

Rabbi Moshe looked at the boy's face, alive with longing. *Truly we are a strange people. Who would have guessed at the depths of religious feeling, the love for the land, in this unlearned boy before me?*

Rabbi Moshe explained that the road to Yerushalayim was long and dangerous, beset by natural perils and wicked men. But the boy insisted that he was used to danger. "And besides," he concluded simply, "what could be safer than traveling with four rabbis?"

At last Rabbi Moshe relented, on the condition that both parents give their permission. As he heard the boy disappear down the hill, crashing through the brush in joyful leaps, Rabbi Moshe wondered if he was right to expose the child to the dangers of such a journey. But what else did Eliezer have before him except a life of uncertainty, of relentless toil and poverty? Could he deny him the sight of the Western Wall, the opportunity to pray at the graves of the Forefathers, when such an experience could be a source of strength, an inspiration throughout his life?

To the end of his days, Rabbi Moshe treasured that journey as the most sacred and happiest time of his life. Thus had their ancestors traveled to the holy city three times a year to bring offerings to the offerings in the *Beit HaMikdash*, to bask in the light of the Divine Presence. He gazed at the faces around him – the fine, spiritual countenance of Rabbi Maimon, the energetic and intelligent face of David, now in the prime of his manhood, the unmarked features and shining eyes of the boy Eliezer – and he knew that they all shared the same dream.

As they neared Yerushalayim, the air became fresher, purer, as the road climbed upward into the hills. Though the land was hilly and desolate, it was planted with vineyards and olive groves. Date trees scattered their sweet fruit upon the earth. The eyes of the travelers were fixed on the mountains rising before them, and they did not pay much heed when one of the Arab guides turned his donkey and veered to the west.

"Why are you going this way?" Rabbi Yafet asked. "Isn't Yerushalayim straight ahead?"

"Don't worry, don't worry," the guide reassured them. He was a short, unkempt man, with shrewd eyes and a drooping mustache. "We will be in the city by nightfall."

They rode for a while through the shadowy woods, the old trees meeting over their heads in a canopy. With every step the forest shut them off more completely from the road. Eliezer, used to the flat plains of Eilat, rode up to Rabbi Moshe and whispered,

"It's dark here, isn't it?" Rabbi Moshe was just turning to reassure him when he saw the two guides turn their donkeys sideways and block the road. They stood facing the travelers, and something gleamed in their hands... the shiny, flat blades of daggers.

Rabbi Yafet and Rabbi Maimon rode up to the guides, with David bringing up the rear. "What is the meaning of this?" Rabbi Yafet demanded in a shaking voice.

"Pay us five hundred silver pieces or you die here." The Arab's sharp, black eyes were hard as coals. His companion, a burly, stupid-looking fellow, just nodded.

"Are you out of your mind? We paid you already!" Rabbi Yafet looked helplessly at David and Moshe.

"Give us the money or you die here, and we will have your donkeys and supplies instead."

"Do you realize what you are doing?" David's voice cut like a knife, and his gentle eyes were dark with anger. "We have warned the authorities that you are taking the Chief Rabbi of Acco and his companions to Yerushalayim. If we do not return, they will be combing the country for you."

"We will say you were slain by the Orbanites," the guide replied indifferently. "Off your donkeys. Now!"

A sudden, heavy rumble made him lift his head. The noise rolled away, and a violent glare fell upon the darkness of the woods. A dazzling burst lit up the old trees and seemed to last for a long time.

At that moment, Eliezer's young voice rang out. "It is the hand of G-d. You dared to harm these holy men." The growl of thunder exploded in a great crash, and the bolt of lightning seemed indeed to have found the robbers. They stood distinct and black against a sea of light, rigid with terror. Then, with a tremendous crash, the darkness leaped back and the figures vanished from their eyes. A terrified shout came from the blackness; there was a loud scuffle, muffled words, and then the sound of retreating hooves.

"I think they have fled," Rabbi Maimon said in a weak but calm voice. "Eliezer spoke well. It was indeed the hand of G-d."

They stood huddled together as sheets of rain descended upon them. The wind tore at the shrubs and shook the tops of the trees. At last, the sky cleared, and the glow of a thousand stars gazed down upon them.

"We must certainly recite *Birchat Hagomel* when we reach Yerushalayim," said Rabbi Moshe, "to give thanks for our miraculous escape."

"But how will we find our way back?" Eliezer asked in a voice that was suddenly small and frightened.

"Do not fear, Eliezer. My two sons are both well versed in the positions of the stars. They will guide us back to the road," Rabbi Maimon assured him.

Exhausted and soaked to the skin, they made their weary way back to the road. Dawn found them in sight of the holy city again. Their fright was quickly forgotten as the sun rose in a silent

*The growl of thunder exploded in a great crash...*

burst of light, illuminating their ascent up the steps that were cut into the side of the Mountain of Olives. Before them lay the *Har Habayit*. The great stones of the Western Wall, all that remained of the *Beit HaMikdash*, stood patient and eternal in the pure light. They seemed to be waiting, dreaming away the centuries, for the moment when the sound of the shofar would rend the air and the dispersed would be gathered from the four corners of the earth.

Rabbi Moshe took hold of his robe and rent it wordlessly. The others followed his example. They prayed there, together with a *minyan* of Jews, as the sun rose in the sky and bathed the stones of the Western Wall in gold. *"Return in mercy to Your city Yerushalayim,"* they whispered, *"and dwell therein as You have promised... rebuild it soon in our days..."*

Two days later they stood in a dark cave in the hills of Chevron. Flares were set in the walls, illuminating the large cavern. Several large stones lay before them, flickering in the torch light. Rabbi Moshe bent forward. "Look," he whispered. They all gathered around him and read in voices hushed with awe: "This is the grave of Avraham our father. Here lies Sara our mother, and here, Yitzchok and Rivka, Yaakov and Leah."

For an entire day, Rabbi Moshe stood and prayed on that spot. He did not hear the others leave softly to wait for him outside. He felt neither thirst nor hunger. "Avraham our father lies buried here," he thought, "Avraham, who has shown us the ultimate level of love and fear of Hashem, who has opened a way for his children to serve the Holy One, Blessed Be He, that is beyond the capacity of human nature."

He thought of the old man, childless for so many years, longing for a son so that he could establish a nation dedicated to the service of G-d. How great had been his love and gratitude when at last a son was granted to him! And yet he was ready to give up this beloved child and hastened to sacrifice him, not with sorrow, but with joy, and not in fear of punishment or hope of reward, but only for love and fear of G-d.

"G-d of Avraham," he whispered with intense concentration, "answer us. Father of Yitzchok, answer us. Mighty One of Yaakov, answer us... Look down, Hashem, and see our desolation..."

When he rejoined the others, his eyes were still far away, and his face seemed to glow with an unfathomable joy.

"Today is a day I shall never forget," he said slowly. "Just as the day of the storm will be marked forever in my memory, so the three glorious days when I stood in the gates of Yerushalayim and prayed at the graves of our Forefathers in Chevron will be Yomim Tovim, days of prayer and rejoicing."[5]

He fell silent and thought for a moment. How could joy be complete when the Temple lay in ruins and the Jewish people were in exile? He sighed. "And just as we were granted the chance to pray in our Holy Land in its destruction and desolation, may we all see it in its consolation, with the coming of Mashiach."

---

[5] Letters of the Rambam in Sefer HaChareidim.

The others all answered, "Amein."

The group parted on the road outside of Chevron. Rabbi Yafet and Eliezer would join a party headed for Eilat and return home. Rabbi Maimon and his two sons would go back to Yerushalayim, for the elderly father was sorely in need of rest, and then...

"And then you will come back to us?" asked the boy, an anxious frown creasing his sunburned face. His arms and legs, too, were smooth and brown, free of scabs.

"No, Eliezer." Rabbi Moshe hesitated a moment. This was not an easy thing to say to the child in whom he had helped to kindle the love of the Holy Land. "I'm afraid we cannot stay here much longer. We will probably travel on to..." He felt a sudden aversion to pronouncing the name of the land that was the very symbol of exile... "to Egypt."

"Egypt?" the boy exclaimed. "But why Egypt? Didn't you tell us that it's a great mitzva to live in *Eretz Yisrael*?" His large eyes regarded his teacher accusingly.

"Eliezer!" Rabbi Yafet lifted an admonishing finger.

"Rabbi Yafet, he has a right to know." Rabbi Moshe put a hand on the boy's shoulder. "Believe me, my son, it is my dearest wish to remain here in *Eretz Yisrael*. If there was any way I could possibly do so, if we could find a way to support ourselves and make a living, we would never leave."

Eliezer did not turn to meet his eyes, but only stared

stubbornly down the road that led to Acco.

"Don't you see, Eliezer, if I remained, I would live on charity, and that I can never do. So we must go where our livelihood leads us.

"And remember, Eliezer," he added softly, "when Jews part, it is only in body. In spirit, we are joined forever."

At last the boy turned to face him. A deep flush rose into his cheeks, spreading across his forehead to the roots of his dark hair. "I'll never forget you, I'll never forget what you taught me. You are the best teacher I ever had. And you took me with you..." His voice choked... "it's the most wonderful thing that ever happened to me in my whole life."

As they rode off toward Yerushalayim, they heard the boy's high, light voice calling, *"L'shanah haba'ah b'Yerushalayim habnuya..."* Next year in Yerushalayim.

They rode on in silence for a while, Rabbi Moshe reviewing in his mind all the reasons for moving to Egypt. It was a prosperous land, one where David could make a living dealing in precious stones. There was a large, established Jewish community that was greatly in need of guidance and leadership. If only...

Suddenly, Rabbi Moshe saw his father sway in the saddle. "Father," he cried out and reached to support him. The old man's face was white as chalk, and beads of sweat stood out on his forehead. His sons settled him under the shade of a tree and pressed the water bag to his lips. "I'm better now, my sons," he said with a smile. "But I am an old man. Come, let us proceed to Yerushalayim."

In the holy city they were welcomed by an elderly couple, friends of Rabbi Yafet. The little, old woman, a white kerchief tied tightly around her head, ran about like a bird, ordering her daughter to prepare the beds, begging them to eat and drink.

Rabbi Moshe and David looked down at their father's pale face anxiously. He lay in the large bed that had been prepared for him. "You will feel better in the morning," they assured him. "Now you can rest."

Rabbi Maimon gazed out of the window, at the azure sky and the hills of Yerushalayim. "Yes," he whispered, "yes, my sons, now I can rest."

It was the last time they spoke to him, for in the morning they found that Rabbi Maimon, the father, scholar, and lover of his people, had gone.

During the week of *shiva*, a steady procession of scholars and simple people passed through the gray stone house. Letters poured in from every corner of the world, comforting the brothers for their great loss.

The universal love and reverence in which their father was held consoled them. "And also," said David, looking out the window at the hills of the city, where their father's last gaze had rested, "after all the flight and fear, after all his wanderings, it was here in Yerushalayim that he returned his soul to his Creator."

## Chapter Ten

# THE FALSE PROPHET

Mazal had been weaving in the cool dimness of the house when she heard Tamar calling, "Come with me, Mazal, I'm going for water!"

Gratefully, Mazal dropped the loom. "May I go?" she asked her mother, who was kneading dough for supper.

"Go ahead, my dear," her mother said absently, then called after her in a sharper tone, "and don't forget what your father said. No going near the mountain."

"I won't, I won't," Mazal promised, grabbing the water pitcher by the door. "We won't be long!"

The courtyard was a blaze of sunshine. High in the blue sky a blackbird hovered. Oh, it was good to be outdoors, free to stroll along the sandy path to the well. And to go with Tamar was doubly delightful, for her cousin always had something exciting to tell her.

The girls linked arms and walked along at a leisurely pace. They looked remarkably alike, easily passing as twins, with their round, dimpled cheeks and large, dark eyes. The one difference between them was that Mazal had silver earrings twinkling in her delicate ears, and Tamar had none. In a fit of enthusiasm, she had given away all her worldly possessions to the poor. It was a foolish thing to do, Mazal's mother had scolded her. It went against the law of the Torah, and it all came from listening to the preaching of the man on the mountain.

"I was in the market today," Tamar began as soon as they were out of earshot of the house. She was an orphan who lived with a series of relatives, going from home to home and helping out wherever she was needed most at the time. Though she did her share of hard work, she was free to come and go as she pleased. "And I saw him, the traitor."

"Ooh," breathed Mazal, giving a little shiver. "The apostate! What did he look like?"

"He is not much to look at, I can tell you that. An ugly little man with a mean yellow face and a hunchback." Tamar scrunched up her straight back to demonstrate. "He smiles at the Muslims, sweet as honey. But when he looks at us, his eyes are like a snake's."

"I heard that he tells terrible lies about us and the Torah," said Mazal, happy that she had something to add to the conversation. "He said that Moshe Rabbeinu wrote in the Torah that Mohammed would take his place and the Jews would follow him, G-d forbid."

"He must be crazy," Tamar said, her eyes round with horror. "Where does it say that in the Torah?"

"Oh, he says it's not there anymore, that we Jews erased it. Can you imagine, erasing a word of the Torah? Why, our Torah is eternal! Not even a crown on any letter has been changed. I heard there is a country far away over the sea, called France, and that the Jews there have a *Sefer Torah* exactly like our own."

"How do you know all this?" Tamar looked at her cousin in surprise, for it was usually she herself who was in possession of new information. "Did your father tell you?"

Mazal nodded. "Do you remember what I told you about that letter that came from a great rabbi? His name is Rabbi Moshe, from Spain, I think, or maybe Egypt. Anyway, he wrote us from far away to teach us what to do in this time of trouble."

"Oh, Rabbi Moshe," Tamar sounded disappointed. At that moment the girls arrived at the well. It was still early, so they sat down on top of the steps leading to the fountain and watched the white water splash on the tiles. "It's because of him that your father won't let you listen to the prophet on the mountain."

"That's right," Mazal fixed her stern eyes on her cousin. "The man on the mountain is just as dangerous as the traitor because he is a false prophet, and a false prophet is a terrible thing. Rabbi Moshe ben Maimon says that he will lead our people astray and bring more troubles upon us, *chas v'shalom.*"

"Oh, but you should see him, Mazal, just once," Tamar cried. "He's so wonderful! He stands on a platform on top of the hill, so tall and noble. His eyes flash, he lifts his arms – so – and he calls, 'Come, let us go forth and meet the Mashiach.' Your father may not believe him," she added defensively, "but lots of people do, hundreds and hundreds, Jews and Muslims also. You don't know how good it feels to see other people honor us and look up to us for once."

"Hush, let's stop arguing." Mazal ran down the steps, scooped up a handful of fresh, cold water, and splashed her cousin in the face. Soon both girls were throwing water at each other. Their hair, blue-black and shiny-wet, dripped into their eyes.

The road curved around the hill, and a hum came from behind the screen of trees. "Listen," Tamar said, standing still as a statue. "The people have gathered. They are waiting for him. I don't care – I'm going!"

"You mustn't, Tamar. Rabbi Moshe said the poor man is crazy. That's why he sees visions and hears voices and thinks Hashem is speaking to him." Mazal saw her friend wavering and renewed her attack. "The real Mashiach will be wise, wiser than any man on the face of the earth, and filled with the spirit of G-d. This man is ignorant and foolish."

A great shout rose up from the mountain. Tamar put down her pitcher at the side of the road and grasped her friend's hands in both of her own. "Listen to me, Mazal. Maybe you are right. Let's just watch one more time. We won't go up on the hill. Do you see this tree?" A large oak rose at the side of the road, lifting its arms to heaven. "Let's climb up. There is a branch that overlooks the meeting place. Come on, just once."

Mazal did not know exactly how it happened, but there they were, sitting comfortably in the fork of a great branch and looking down through a cluster of leaves at a crowd of people gathered on the hilltop.

Tamar was right. It was a mixed crowd, Jews and Muslims, many women and children, and even a few scholarly men with gray beards and clean white robes. Then she saw him. He was standing on a makeshift platform, a tall, broad-shouldered figure in a robe as blue as the sky. He lifted a commanding arm, and the hillside grew quiet. A baby cried briefly, and its mother hushed it.

"My dear children," echoed a ringing voice, "for you are all children of G-d, whether Jew or Muslim..."

Tamar squeezed her cousin's hand tightly. "That's him. Isn't he wonderful?"

"I am here today to reveal to you a great secret." An excited hum rippled through the crowd. The man waited for silence. "I have come to reveal the identity of the Mashiach we have all been waiting and longing for."

"It's you, it's you!" the roar swept through the crowd. "Long live the Mashiach, son of David! Long live the king!"

Suddenly a clear, sharp sound rent the air, a great trumpet blast. "The shofar, the shofar!" the crowd cried.

"Mazal, Mazal, it's the shofar. The shofar of Mashiach!" Tamar hugged her cousin tightly, almost upsetting her balance. Mazal clung to the branch, breathless. The sound was repeated, and a battalion of soldiers marched into sight. They were Ethiopians, black as the night, dressed in brilliant scarlet uniforms.

*He lifted a commanding arm, and the hillside grew quiet.*

"Oh, it wasn't the shofar of Mashiach," sighed Tamar, pointing to the gold trumpets in the hands of two soldiers. "But look, I think those are the guards of the Prince."

The crowd parted then, and the soldiers took their position in two straight lines, facing each other. A black horse appeared, led by an Arab slave dressed in white. Two others, similarly dressed, approached the horse and with great care eased a man of immense bulk onto the ground. He was dressed in rich, colored silk and gold embroidery. His huge head was enfolded in a green turban that glittered with precious stones.

"The Prince, the Prince." A respectful murmur swept the crowd.

"He, too, has come to see the Mashiach," whispered Tamar. "Isn't this wonderful, Mazal? Aren't you glad you came?"

Slowly, deliberately, the prince lifted his bull-like head. A voice, hoarse and powerful as distant thunder, demanded, "Who among you is the man who claims to be the Messiah?"

The prophet stepped forward, his head held fearlessly high. "It is I, my lord."

The girls could see his expression, the proud flash of his eyes. Behind him the western sky was a blaze of crimson.

"And you claim to all these people that you have been sent by G-d to redeem the Jewish nation?"

"That is so, my lord."

"If it is so, then give me a sign." The Prince's voice was a low rumble, commanding but not unfriendly.

"A sign, a sign," the crowd murmured, "he wants a sign."

"Prove to me that you are the prophet of G-d, and I too will follow you."

Mazal was looking down upon the prophet at that moment. His face had changed; a quick grimace – was it fear? – distorted his features, but he answered in a ringing voice, "I am ready, my lord, and here is my sign. "Cut off my head," the proud voice declared. "Cut it off, and I will rise again, alive and well."

"Oh, the poor man! He wants his head cut off!" Tamar's dark eyes were shocked. "He is crazy, you were right. Oh, someone has to stop him. He is going to get killed!" Mazal's heart was beating like a drum. Her only thought was, "Oh, no, I shouldn't have stayed. I should have listened to my mother. Why did I stay?"

The prince lifted his massive head and gave a small nod to his soldiers. Two crimson-clad guards stepped forward and marched firmly toward the man in blue. Swords glittered in their black hands.

The girls clung to each other in terror and with bowed heads whispered the *Shema*: "*Shema Yisrael Hashem Elokeinu, Hashem Echad.*"

In the terrible silence they heard the wail of a baby, and then the high, thin voice of a child. "He isn't getting up. He said he would get up."

Fearfully, Mazal peaked through her fingers. A crumpled heap of blue lay upon the platform.

Slowly, ponderously, the prince turned his immense bulk toward the crowd. Mazal saw that his heavy face was furrowed with rage. "A sign!" he roared contemptuously, his furious little eyes raking the crowd. "This was his sign? You Jews, you will pay for this! You have made fools of yourselves, and of our people." Suddenly the Ethiopians broke their formation and charged into the crowd, their glittering swords raised.

There was a great panic. Hundreds of terrified voices combined to make a sound like the screeching of the wind in a storm. A woman's wail rose above the din: "My baby... my baby..."

In an agony of fear, the girls scrambled down from the tree. Mazal felt her skirt catch on a branch. For a moment she hung suspended between earth and sky. At last the hem ripped, and she fell heavily onto her knee. Crying, the girls ran toward the road, the din of the panic-stricken crowd echoing behind them.

Twilight lay over the village as they ran, the earth flying backward beneath their feet. Sobbing and gasping, they burst through the gate and into the sheltering arms of Mazal's parents.

Mazal buried her head in her mother's comforting shoulder, crying uncontrollably. Tamar was beside her, clinging to her aunt silently.

"He didn't get up," Mazal gasped at last. "The people were screaming. Rabbi Moshe was right, he was right! I'm sorry..."

*"He didn't get up," Mazal gasped at last.*

"We know, daughter, we know." Her father was not even angry. "We know all that happened. Thank G-d you are both safe! Many Jews lost their lives today, and there will be more trouble to come."

"It's over, Tamar, it's over," her aunt said soothingly, trying to comfort the sobbing child. "Don't cry anymore."

Tamar lifted her tear-stained face. "And I gave away my earrings and bracelet... all for nothing." Mazal put an arm around her cousin's shoulder.

Mazal's father rose and began rummaging in the cedar chest, where the family's few possessions were kept. He returned with a roll of parchment, which he unfolded slowly and reverently.

"Listen, my children. We must not despair. These are the words of Rabbi Moshe ben Maimon. David the scribe made me a copy." He found the place he was seeking and began to read: "And these are the words foretold by our prophets, that as the days of Mashiach approach, many will arise and argue that they are Mashiach, but their claims will not be fulfilled, and they will be lost, and many will be lost with them.

"But the Creator of the world will remember us in His great mercy and will gather together His people, His inheritance, to look upon His glory and to visit in His house. And He will take us out from this valley of the shadow of death and remove the darkness from our eyes and hearts."[6]

The mother lit a candle, for it had grown dark, and the

[6] Iggeret Taiman, Rabbi Moshe ben Maimon.

flickering light illuminated the sober faces of the family. The father's voice was low but full of hope. "And Hashem will shine upon you, and His glory will be revealed to you."

In his spacious home in Cairo, Rabbi Moshe ben Maimon received the letter from Yemen during the midday meal. His wife sat opposite him with the children, one small head at her shoulder, the other at her side. It was the only opportunity Rabbi Moshe had during the day to spend a few moments with his family, and at these times he tried to give them his full attention. He had waited too long for a home, for children of his own, to regard this blessing lightly.

He glanced at the letter briefly. What he read caused a smile of great happiness to lighten his solemn countenance. He would share the good tidings with his wife. She deserved to hear it, for she suffered much on his account. He knew that she lived in constant fear that his enemies would slander him, that something he had written, perhaps years ago, would be found subversive and disrespectful by the rulers of the land, and that he would be taken from her and the children, never to return, G-d forbid.

"Look, my dear wife, this is a letter from Yemen. Do you remember how you begged me not to get involved, how afraid you were? Listen and you will see that no harm can come to us when we are working for the good of our people. Listen to the words of the letter:

"'And behold, I call to witness heaven and earth that we

have heard from men of truth, that in all the lands of Yemen many communities are engaged in the learning of Torah and the performance of good deeds for the sake of Heaven.'"

He looked up to find her smiling, rejoicing in his happiness. "It seems the persecutions have eased as well, that our efforts in the Caliph's court have borne fruit. Our Caliph is a good man, fair and just. The princes of Yemen seem to have heeded his warning to treat their Jewish subjects more fairly."

He turned the page to read further, but then fell silent and astonished. Tears filled his eyes, for the Jews of Yemen had accorded him an honor that had never yet been granted to a living human being. In their gratitude, they had bestowed a gift upon him that he would cherish to the end of his days.

"In all the communities of Yemen," the letter read, "the name of Rabbi Moshe ben Maimon is mentioned in the *Kaddish* prayer, in every service, as follows: 'May He bring forth the Redemption and hasten the coming of Mashiach, in your days and in your lifetime and in the lifetime of Rabbi Moshe ben Maimon.' For he illuminated their eyes to Torah and placed them in a beam of light, to remove from them cruel decrees and the burden of taxes; and he made light the burden of exile."[7]

---

[7] Letter of the Rambam to Chachmei Tzarfat printed in Sefer Mitzaret Chachma.

## Chapter Eleven

# HE WAS MY BROTHER

Rabbi Maimon bent over his work, his quill moving steadily over the parchment. Behind him was a window open to the dark night and clear stars. The large table before him was strongly lit by the flame of a large candle and strewn with scrolls and books, some open, some closed. The other corners of the spacious apartment were lost shapeless shadows.

Four years had passed since Rabbi Moshe had moved to Egypt. They had been hard years, beset with trials. His face, now bent intently over his work, had grown thinner, and the broad forehead had become webbed with fine lines. Here and there a silver thread appeared in his dark beard.

It was very quiet in the room. The only sound was the sputtering of the candle and the dry scratching of pen on parchment. Rabbi Moshe lifted his head for a moment; he knew not why. Was he still listening for high peals of childish laughter, for a pair of light and purposeful footsteps? He sighed and bent again over his scroll. *Baruch Hashem* there was work to be done, enough to occupy every waking hour. The giant task, the commentary on the Mishna, was almost complete. How many years had he been working on it? It had wandered with him from one end of the world to the other, over Spanish mountains and the foaming ocean, from Morocco to the Holy Land. And at last, here in Fostat, G-d willing, it would be completed.

He hoped to finish it soon, for it was badly needed. The faithful Jews would have a guide to understanding the Mishna and how the laws were derived from it. It would be, he hoped, an introduction to the study of the Talmud as well. And what of the Karaites, his erring brothers, who had shaken off the yoke of the Mishna and the Talmud, claiming that all they needed were the Five Books of Moses? Perhaps they, too, would come to see in time that the Mishna and the Talmud were essential for the performance of the mitzvot, that the Torah was one and indivisible, every word of it holy and binding, and that Moshe Rabbeinu had been given an Oral Law along with the Written Law on Sinai.

The Karaites. Rabbi Moshe shook his head in perplexity. Their behavior flew in the face of simple common sense. Wishing to throw off the yoke of tradition, the teachings of the sages and the burden of the mitzvot, had they made life any sweeter? The Shabbat, a day of rest and joy, they had turned into a dark and cheerless day. Misinterpreting the verse, "You shall light no fires in your dwelling places," they sat all Shabbat in cold, dark homes, denying themselves the cheerful crackle of a fire, the comfort of a warm meal. Yes, they even forbade the lighting of Shabbat candles by Jewish mothers and daughters.

Suddenly, with a piercing clarity, he saw his wife standing before the Shabbat candles, white hands outstretched over the flames, whose dancing reflection was mirrored in the eyes of his son and daughter. Within a month, all precious three of them had been taken from him during the terrible plague that had swept Egypt. The two children had been buried on the same day. Neither his prayers nor his knowledge of medicine had been able to save them.

Rabbi Moshe shook his head. This was not the right way. Not to mourn at all was cruel and callous, but to mourn too much showed lack of faith in the Holy One, Blessed Be He. Surely, these three pure souls had fulfilled their purpose here on earth and had found their resting place in the world that was all good. But what was one to do with the terrible loneliness that gripped the heart like an invisible hand?

Thank G-d, he still had his brother. David stood beside him always, a source of comfort and strength. He had been gone for many weeks now on a journey to India, where his trade in diamonds had taken him; he had gone to face the hazards of the open seas so that Moshe could sit over his books in this peaceful study. Rabbi Moshe's thoughts now navigated with his brother, flowing between the reefs of the Sea of Rushes toward the open spaces of the Indian Ocean. Perhaps, if David's venture were successful, he would be able to settle down after all his years as a wandering merchant, open a business, and stay near his wife and baby daughter.

They would have more time to learn together, he mused. What a joy it would be to watch David's keen mind, so like their holy father's, sail on the sea of the Talmud instead of tossing on stormy waves.

There was a sharp rap on the door. The sound was startling in the quiet room at that late hour. His servants were long asleep, so Rabbi Moshe rose to admit the unexpected visitor.

The man who stood in the doorway was no vagabond. He was a well-dressed merchant in his middle years, tall and solidly built. But his manner was distraught and uncertain.

"Rabbi, I saw the candle..."

Rabbi Moshe drew him into the study and invited him to be seated, but the man shook his head mutely. Now that he had entered the circle of light, it was clear that he was in the grip of some powerful emotion. The large hands resting on the table trembled, and a thin film of perspiration covered his pale, troubled face.

"Come, my friend," Rabbi Moshe said gently. "Tell me what troubles you. We are alone, you can speak freely ."

"Rabbi Moshe, I am a partner with your brother David."

Rabbi Moshe rose, alarmed. The candle flared like a ghostly torch beneath the merchant's white face. "It's bad news that I bring you..."

Further words were unnecessary. He knew then that there was no hope, no reprieve, that all was lost. In a hoarse voice, the man continued to relate how the ship had gone down in a hurricane with all aboard, one hundred souls and a treasure in

*"It's bad news that I bring you..."*

pearls and precious stones.

A sudden pain shot through Rabbi Moshe, as though lightning had rent his chest. "*Baruch Dayan HaEmet* – Blessed is the True Judge," he whispered. The room was dark. Had the candle gone out? From far away, from the bottom of a deep well in which he seemed to have fallen, he heard the man asking, "Is there anything I can do? Anyone else to tell?"

Rabbi Moshe pressed his head between his hands, struggling to clear his mind. "Yes, yes, there is a young wife and a baby girl. And I have one sister remaining, Miriam. She is married, here, in Fostat." What else was there? There was something else. "And the money entrusted to him, by you and others – after the *shiva* we will inform them – they will be repaid."

Soon he sat alone on the low stool of the mourner. From the adjoining room he could hear the soft weeping of David's young wife and of Miriam, his sister. Once again, the scholars and merchants, the simple people of Egypt passed before him, offering their words of comfort. And he, who believed so much in the power of speech, wanted to tell them about his brother David's love for Torah, of his valiant, fearless spirit and generous heart. But for once, words failed him. Only years later, in a letter to his friend Rabbi Yafet in Eilat, would he be able to express the enormity of his loss.

"In Egypt I met with great and severe misfortunes, but the most terrible blow that befell me, a blow which caused me more grief than anything I have ever experienced in my life, was the death of the *tzaddik*, who was drowned while traveling across the Indian Ocean. Eight years have since passed, and I still mourn for him and cannot be comforted. And how shall I be comforted? For he was a son to me, who grew up on my knee. He was my brother, my pupil. He engaged himself in business so that I could stay home, engrossed in my studies. My one joy was to see him. Now my joy has been changed into darkness. He has gone to his eternal home and has left me alone in a strange land.

"And even now, when I come across his handwriting or one of his books, my heart grows faint within me, and my grief is reawakened. Were it not for the Torah, my delight, I would have perished in my suffering."[8]

As a physician, Rabbi Moshe had always believed that the health of mind and body were closely connected. After this last great blow to his spirit, it seemed that his body, too, turned against him. Directly after the *shiva*, he fell into a sickbed and did not rise for nearly a year. He lay on his tumbled bed, twisting and turning in fever and pain, fighting for breath. He, who had often ministered to others, now watched doctors come and go, gravely shaking their heads. At times a great weariness overcame him, and the longing for peace became stronger than the will to live. At these times, he seemed to hear his father's voice: "My son, you must guard your life!"

So he fought on, to the sound of his drumming heart and rasping breath.

[8] Michtav L'Rabbi Yafet HaDayan by the Rambam.

*...the longing for peace became stronger than the will to live.*

One morning, the pain began to recede like the tide going out. Breath came more easily. At last he was able to stand by the open window and look down into the courtyard. The mist had risen, and the garden lay before him, fresh and innocent, like a little child. A cool breeze blew in through the open window, bearing the fragrance of peach blossoms.

The trees were blooming in the courtyard, and a small girl with jet-black curls alternately walked and skipped around the fountain, singing a song of her own invention. *It was David's little daughter,* he realized with a pang, *and she was no longer a baby.* Rabbi Moshe lifted his eyes to the pale blue canopy of the sky and murmured, "I offer thanks to You, living and eternal King, for You have mercifully restored my soul within me."

The small girl turned a laughing face up to him and waved. How like her father she looked! Tears filled Rabbi Moshe's eyes. David was gone. It was his turn to care for the child and her mother, to shoulder the burden of supporting the family. But what could he do? The life of commerce was not for him, of that he was certain. The leaders of the community had repeatedly offered to pay him for teaching in the yeshiva, sitting on the Rabbinical Court, and giving lectures, but that too was impossible; for it was written in the Mishna, "Whoever derives personal gain from the words of Torah removes his life from the world!" No, he would have to be self-sufficient and live by the sweat of his brow if necessary.

Suddenly, his face cleared. Medicine. He would practice

the profession he had learned in Morocco. He smiled a little, recalling the fat physician who had taught him well. He would have to review, of course, and study the latest developments in medicine. Of one thing he was sure. He would never turn away a patient who could not pay the fee. Were not all people G-d's creatures, who shared the sight of the stars, the warmth of the sun?

Softly he murmured a prayer which became the creed of all doctors dedicated to the relief of human suffering: "I ready myself to practice my craft. Help me, oh G-d, in my task. Fill my heart with love for Your creatures. Do not allow the love of gain or hunger for fame to tarnish the purity of my actions. Strengthen the powers of my body and soul, to be ever ready to help the rich and the poor, the good and the bad, friend or foe. Let me see in the sick man only Your creature, a human being."[9]

---

[9] T'filat HaRofeh, attributed to the Rambam.

## Chapter Twelve

# A CURE FOR THE EYES

Rabbi Avraham Ibn Ezra knocked impatiently on the imposing cedar door of the fine house in Fostat. He had come all the way from Spain to visit the Rambam, but now that he had arrived, he saw it was no easy matter to gain an audience with the great man.

His knock was answered by the same round-faced Muslim who had turned him away yesterday and the day before. Once again the servant explained that his master was gone for the day.

"Again?" Rabbi Avraham demanded. His feet ached in their broken shoes, and his stomach rumbled with hunger. "I have been here morning and evening for the past three days. Is your master ever home?"

The polite servant shook his head. "My master leaves the house at the crack of dawn every day to travel to the Caliph's palace in Cairo. He is the physician of the entire royal family. He does not return until late afternoon." He looked the visitor up and down, from his frayed turban to his broken shoes. "We have a dining room for wayfarers," he offered tactfully, "and if it is a donation..."

Rabbi Ibn Ezra shook his head. Even this Arab servant had

found him out, he thought a little ruefully. He might fancy himself a poet and a scholar, but in the eyes of the world he was just another poor man. And if the truth be told, if he were completely honest with himself, had he really come all this way merely to bask in the brilliance of the Rambam and to be enlightened by his wisdom? Had he not hoped, somewhere in the back of his mind, that this successful and fabulously generous fellow scholar would give him a fitting gift and thereby ease the bitter poverty that pursued him like a shadow?

"No, thank you," he replied firmly. "It is your master I wish to see, not his coins."

As the door closed in his face, he had a stroke of inspiration. Bending, he scooped up a bit of chalk, and scrawled across the imposing gate:

*I arise early to see the prince,*

*They say he rode away;*

*I return at evening tide,*

*He has retired for the day.*

*Either he lies in his bed,*

*Or he has ridden far,*

*Alas for this poor man,*

*Born without a star.* [10]

A mischievous smile tugged at his weary face. "Let us see if my wise friend will recognize the author." There was nothing

[10] from a poem attributed to Rabbi Avraham Ibn Ezra.

left to do but to return in the afternoon, and to while away the time until then with a bit of shade and a drink of water to still his hunger.

When he returned in the late afternoon, the servant with the nut-brown face regarded him severely. "You are the one who scribbled on the door," he said, pointing an accusing finger. "My master saw it."

"He did?" Rabbi Avraham smiled. "Was he annoyed?"

The servant shook a puzzled head. "He laughed. I have never seen him laugh before. But you can't see him now. He is busy with patients and cannot be disturbed."

Again no entry. The Ibn Ezra thought fast and then put his foot in the doorway. "I too am in need of his help," he said quickly. If this was the only way to get the great man's attention, so be it. "Where do I go if I need medical attention?"

The servant looked at him suspiciously. "Well, if you are sick, you walk along the side of the building. The clinic is in the back."

He did not have to search for long. Around the corner, a straggling line of humanity was waiting patiently to be admitted to the clinic. Men who seemed quite hale and hearty, wrinkled old couples shaking with age, small boys with fearless eyes, little girls with long, tumbling hair, and women embracing sleeping babies all streamed through the open door. The continuous shuffling line spilled from one large waiting room into another, a mixture of people of all walks of life, both Jewish and Muslim.

Many had horrible sores on their bodies. Others were obviously weak from fever. A few who were very ill lay on stretchers, guarded by worried relatives.

Avraham Ibn Ezra was finally assigned a cot by a courteous attendant. All around him patients waited for the doctor, dozing or talking quietly. Suddenly, there was a stir. An excited murmur passed through the crowded room. "The Doctor! The Doctor is coming."

Rabbi Avraham raised himself on one elbow and regarded the Rambam. The famous physician was not a tall man, and his broad shoulders were slighty stooped. He walked through the crowd with a calm, steady tread. Immediately, Rabbi Avraham was impressed by the feeling of great power behind the quiet reserve. He saw a steadfast purity of purpose on the gentle face. "Ahh," he sighed to himself, "the world is not mistaken. Here is a great man in Israel."

The Rambam stopped by every cot and listened to each patient with intense concentration, whether he was a beggar in a tattered robe or a richly-clad official. "It seems," thought Rabbi Avraham, "as if no other person in the world exists for him but the one in front of him."

At last his own turn came, and he felt the intensity of that searching gaze. Avraham had a sudden, sharp pang of fear. How had he dared to trifle with this wise man, to pretend illness and play such foolish games? The penetrating gaze seemed to go through him, to see him entirely, to see his suffering and need.

With relief, he saw that the eyes were warm and compassionate. The grave lips twitched slightly; the heavy eyebrows lifted a drop. Slowly he nodded his head and scribbled something on the pad in his hand. Then he was off, bending attentively toward the next patient.

"Ah, he knows me," mused Rabbi Avraham Ibn Ezra. "He has seen right through me." He turned to a wrinkled old Jew beside him and asked, "Can you tell me what happens next, my friend? It's the first time I have been here."

The old man was happy to enlighten him. In a few hours the attendants would return, bringing the prescriptions the doctor had prepared for them, along with detailed instructions. The Rambam did not like to impose on his patients the way other doctors did, and seldom made them return the following day for their medication.

"If you searched from one end of the earth to the other, you would find no one like him," added the old man. "He is also a great scholar, a rabbi in the community. He has a yeshiva and supports the poor. They say he has written books as well, but that does not sound possible unless, of course, he is an angel and not a man."

Exactly as the old man had predicted, the attendants in the spotless white robes returned in the evening. One carried a basket heaped high with medications, and the other read from a list the names of the patients and the appropriate instructions.

They stopped by Rabbi Avraham's cot, and the young man

with the list began reading, "Give Avraham Ibn Ezra...

He paused with a slight, squinted at the instructions, and then drew his companion aside for a whispered consultation. At last he read aloud with a puzzled shrug, "Please give this sick man a note to draw four hundred silver pieces from my treasury, and he will be cured."

"Take this note," continued the attendant, turning to Rabbi Avraham, "to the treasurer of the Rambam, and he will do as he is instructed."

Rabbi Avraham walked through the streets of Fostat, which were now unfamiliar in the darkness. The moon was a silver crescent sailing before him. This great man, the Rambam, had indeed penetrated to the heart of his problem, his incurable poverty. Yes, that was his disease, the poverty that had dogged his footsteps from his youth. Had he not tried every profession under the sun in an attempt to earn his bread honorably, by the sweat of his brow? But somehow when he engaged in a craft that brought a decent living to others, he was always left more destitute than before. Everyone knew his poem:

> *If I were to sell candles,*
>
> *The sun would never set*
>
> *And if I sold shrouds and winding cloths*
>
> *There would be no dead.*[11]

And now his children were grown. He had daughters of marriageable age, and he had been reduced to a traveling beggar.

[11] from a poem attributed to Rabbi Avraham Ibn Ezra.

What other alternative did he have... to watch his wife cry her eyes out because her daughters sat at home, unable to marry for want of a dowry?

And the Rambam had read his need, his bitterness, as clearly as if it had been written across his face. That was what he was famed for, Rabbi Avraham remembered, for diagnosing an illness by looking into a sick man's eyes. But now he was more determined than ever to become acquainted with this extraordinary man. He would not be content with any sum, even such a princely gift, without a private interview.

To the exasperation of the intelligent young Jew who managed the Rambam's treasury, Avraham refused to accept the silver pieces that had been "prescribed" to him. "I will accept nothing," he kept repeating, "unless it is from the hands of your master himself."

The young treasurer sat silent for a few moments, biting his lips in vexation. It was clear that he was very reluctant to disturb his master. Finally he got up and walked out. Moments later he returned, his manner changed to eager courtesy.

"Please follow me, sir. Rabbi Moshe ben Maimon awaits you."

It was quite a simple room he entered, free of the rich mosaics and elegant tapestries that adorned the rest of the building. The Rambam sat behind a large desk, piled high with parchment scrolls. A space had been cleared before him, and he was eating his evening meal.

"Rabbi Avraham Ibn Ezra!" He rose to greet his visitor with a warm smile. "Please forgive me, but it's the first time I have eaten today. You, too, I fear have not eaten for many hours. Patrus!"

A servant appeared on silent feet. He had the dark face of an Arab, with quick, intelligent eyes.

"Please bring my honored guest from Spain something on which to make a blessing."

The Rambam turned back to Avraham, his face glowing with warmth and pleasure. A smile tugged at the grave lips. "Forgive me for not seeing you until now... except briefly. You do not know what a pleasure it is for me to speak to a scholar from Spain, my old home. But, as you have already seen recorded on my door, my day begins at dawn and ends after midnight. And these moments are my only respite."

Rabbi Avraham Ibn Ezra's heart smote him, for the great physician did not look a well man. He saw the pallor and exhaustion on his face, the dark shadows under his eyes. "Forgive me for insisting," he murmured, "but I have traveled so far, and I could not bear to leave this land without getting to know the one who is called 'the bright light, the shining star who returned our faith to its glory.'"

The Rambam shook his head impatiently. "So much needs to be done. Fences need to be mended, laws need to be clarified. Unfortunately, Shabbat is the only day that I have time to learn Torah and to teach people. The rest of the week I am busy with my patients." He pointed to two baskets piled high with medication. "And for this exacting craft of mine, many hours of preparation and research are required. A human life may hang in the balance.

"My friend, there is no easy way," he continued with compassion. "For one, it is poverty and need. For another, endless labor and the yoke of a livelihood." Avraham Ibn Ezra nodded. He knew the words were meant for him, to help him accept his lot. "Our life in exile is full of troubles and worries and burdens, and none of us can be entirely free of them until the coming of the Redeemer."

Avraham Ibn Ezra saw that, indeed, success had made life no easier for the *tzaddik* before him. Yet he could not resist asking, "But surely, being the private physician of the Caliph himself, of the whole royal family – isn't that a wonderful thing, a great honor for a Jew?"

Rabbi Moshe shook his head slowly and emphatically. "Believe me, my friend, nothing could be further from the truth. A Jew's association with those who are great and powerful brings little joy and much sorrow. Daily, the other doctors and officers scheme with the most bitter envy and hatred to discredit a Jew in the eyes of the Caliph. Many times I have been at the brink of death, G-d forbid, and have been saved only by the mercies of Hashem."[12]

Rabbi Avraham listened in dismay. He was burning to ask why the Rambam did not surrender his perilous position at the

---

[12] Seder Hadorot

Caliph's court and content himself with his private practice. But he had asked too much already, and his courage failed him.

"You wonder why I continue to serve the Caliph," smiled the Rambam. "I wonder too, very often. I can assure you that the only reason I stay on is because once in a while I have the opportunity to gain the ears of the Caliph and sway him, perhaps, to lighten the heavy burdens of our People."

Rabbi Avraham stared at the holy face before him in a daze. Was this the life he had envied, a life of toil and peril and self-sacrifice?

Rabbi Moshe seemed to sense his visitor's thoughts once again, for he turned the conversation to other topics. He questioned him closely about the Jewish communities he had seen in his travels. He told him how very much he enjoyed his poetry and his commentaries, encouraged him to keep on writing, and even quoted his own favorite lines.

The Rambam rose after reciting the *Birchat HaMazon* and excused himself. Unfortunately, there were still patients waiting for him.

"I leave you in the hands of my faithful servant, Patrus. He will give you the freedom of my home. Ask him for anything you need. I fear I will not be able to spend as much time with you as I would like, but rest and refresh yourself." With a courteous nod, he was gone – to work, Avraham Ibn Ezra was certain, into the early hours of the morning.

Rabbi Avraham spent the rest of the week in the spacious

house of the Rambam. Though he caught only glimpses of the great man, he felt a growing closeness to him as he sat reading the books in his wonderful library and speaking to the many people whose lives he had touched. In all of them, from the scholars and leaders of the community to his pretty little orphaned niece, the Rambam seemed to evoke the same emotion – a fierce devotion touched by awe.

It was on Shabbat morning after the *tefillot* that Rabbi Avraham was at last able to listen to the Rambam teach Torah. The majority of the congregation gathered in the courtyard of the house; Jews from every walk of life and every level of scholarship, had come to drink in the words of the great teacher. Ibn Ezra sat spellbound by the discourse of the master.

For this alone, it had been worth traveling to Egypt. Never had he felt more poignantly the truth expressed in the *Tehillim* of David Hamelech: "The Torah of Hashem is perfect, restoring the soul... The mitzva of Hashem is clear, enlightening the eye... They are more desirable than gold... sweeter than honey."

All too soon, the wonderful lesson was over. The members of the community dispersed to their homes for the Shabbat meal, and the Rambam conducted a sumptuous table for a great crowd of traveling scholars, yeshiva students, and simple poor people. During the meal, Rabbi Avraham found out that Rabbi Moshe would speak again in the afternoon. In this session, which was open to anyone who wished to attend, the leaders of the community would bring up pressing problems that faced the Jews of Egypt, and the Rambam would instruct them how to handle that week's difficulties.

The meeting was held in the Rambam's library. A much smaller group gathered there, composed mainly of eminent rabbis and scholars with flowing white beards.

The most pressing issue, Rabbi Avraham discovered, was the problem of the Karaites and how the rabbis should react to them. These Jews, many of whom were rich and powerful, scoffed at Jewish traditions, rejecting the decisions of the sages and making up their own laws as they pleased. How could the rabbis prevent the spread of these heretical ideas among the common people?

Rabbi Moshe ben Maimon rose, and Avraham Ibn Ezra now saw a different man standing before him. Gone was the gentle scholar, and instead there stood before him a warrior of Hashem. With flashing eyes, the Rambam declared war on all those who challenged the laws of the Torah.

His voice rang out in the quiet room. "We must not allow our community to crumble from within. Do not say we have no power, that we are in exile. We have the power invested in us, as the *Bet Din* of this city, a power given us by the Almi-ghty G-d to defend His Torah."

"And if they do not listen?" asked one of the rabbis. "What if they ignore us and mock our authority? They have flagrantly ignored the laws of Jewish marriage and family purity. And we are helpless. What can we do?"

"We are not helpless." Rabbi Moshe fixed stern eyes on

Gone was the gentle scholar, and instead
there stood before him a warrior of Hashem.

the crowd. "Jewish marriage is the very foundation of our existence as a people. Those who wish to destroy it will be excommunicated – with all due force, over *Sifrei Torah*, in every synagogue in Egypt."

There was an excited murmur at these grim words.

"And what about divorce? What if a woman received a *get* from a Karaite synagogue?"

"The divorce is invalid," came the unmoving voice. "She is still married in every sense of the word, and she may not remarry until she receives a divorce sanctioned by a Torah-observant rabbi."

There was a sudden burst of questions.

"Are we permitted to attend their circumcisions? To visit their homes? To invite them to our own? To celebrate with them, rejoice with them, comfort them in their mourning?"

"Absolutely! We may do all of these things!" the Rambam insisted emphatically. "We must share their joys and sorrows, help their poor, support their widows and orphans. We must deal with them in ways of pleasantness and peace."

The puzzled murmuring that followed rose to an excited roar. Rabbi Moshe silenced the crowd with a raised hand. "Why are you surprised? Aren't they our brothers, children of Avraham, Yitzchak, and Yaakov?" His stern voice softened. "We must restrain them with our left hand, but draw them close with our right. And in the end, they will surely return to cherish their inheritance."

The following morning after that wonderful Shabbat, Rabbi Avraham awoke with a sharp, stinging pain in his eyes. He tried to ignore his discomfort by strolling in the courtyard under the shade of the peach trees, but the pain drove him inside. He soaked his eyes in cold water and then in warm, but the pain steadily increased.

By evening, the whites of his eyes had turned a blood red. He had no choice, he realized, but to disturb his benefactor again.

Rather hesitantly, he stood before Rabbi Moshe's desk. Perhaps he should have taken his turn with the other patients in the clinic instead of infringing on his host's precious free time.

Rabbi Moshe looked up at him briefly and then continued poring over his book. Rabbi Avraham explained his reason for coming and described the pain in eyes. But his host made no sign that he had heard him.

He stood and waited in front of the Rambam's desk, abashed as a schoolboy. *This time I have overstepped my bounds he berated himself. I have annoyed this patient man, who has been so kind to me.*

The silence in the room grew unbearable. At last the Rambam lifted his eyes, but only to look at Patrus. "Patrus," he said in a voice that was completely devoid of feeling, "take this man to his room. I do not wish to see him."

Rabbi Avraham returned to his room and paced the floor, distraught and bewildered. How could such total rejection follow so much kindness? The humiliation was hard enough to bear.

But it was the sudden loneliness, the cruel loss of a friendship that had come to mean so much to him, which plunged him into despair.

Bitterly, helplessly, he wept through the night. He tried to control himself because the salty tears burned his aching eyes, but to no avail. The well of tears, sprung from a lifetime of hardship and suffering, erupted within him and flowed on without respite.

The fault, he knew, was in himself. He had seen enough of the Rambam to know that he was a *tzaddik*, perfectly just and kind. Somehow the great rabbi had found him out, penetrated to the core of his unworthiness. He had been smitten in the eyes, Rabbi Avraham reasoned, because his eyes had been wanting. Hadn't he always bemoaned his lot, chafed at his poverty? Perhaps, without knowing it, he had been guilty of a "bad eye," of begrudging Rabbi Moshe Ben Maimon his fame and greatness? And the wise man, with his penetrating vision, had seen his failing and sent him away.

Throughout the entire night he brooded sleeplessly, the tears streaming unchecked from his aching eyes. Then, just as dawn turned the window a pearly gray, there came a knock at the door.

"Come in," he mumbled listlessly.

Into the room, with hands outstretched and a face glowing with kindness and compassion, walked the Rambam.

Startled, Avraham Ibn Ezra rose from his bed. "Rabbi

Throughout the entire night he brooded sleeplessly,
the tears streaming unchecked from his aching eyes.

Moshe..." he stammered, "forgive me..."

"No, no," protested the Rambam, taking both his hands. "I am the one who must ask your forgiveness."

The Ibn Ezra stood astonished as the Rambam explained.

"You see, when you came to me last night, I took one look at your eyes and I realized they were badly infected. A condition like that, G-d forbid, could lead to complications. There is only one cure for this condition known to us, and that is the constant rinsing of the eye in salt water – the salt water of one's tears. I am sorry that I had to cause you pain. And tell me, how are your eyes now?"

"My eyes?" the Ibn Ezra asked in confusion. He had forgotten his pain in the joy of reconciliation. "My eyes . . . why, I feel no pain!" A wide smile spread across his haggard face. "I think they are cured, *Baruch Hashem!*"

The Rambam nodded his head in satisfaction. "The infection has been rinsed away, thank G-d." Then, with a warm smile, he blessed him. "May they be the last tears you are forced to shed. Let only joy and peace be your lot henceforth."

"And may Hashem give him strength," murmured Rabbi Avraham, as the door closed behind his doctor, friend, and teacher, "and lengthen his days."

## Chapter Thirteen

# A FAILED PLOT

"I trust Your Majesty has met with great success in the campaign in the Holy Land." Muhammed's voice was smooth, his manner respectful.

"Yes, yes, all is well." The Caliph regarded the slim and elegant man before him impatiently. As always, his chief adviser was beautifully dressed in a green silk robe and matching turban. Not for him the dust and heat of battle. No, Muhammed always remained behind in the comfort and luxury of the capital city, scheming busily all the while. "You wished to see me, Muhammed?"

"Yes, Sire, there are matters of great importance that I feel..."

"Well, get on with it, get on with it," the Caliph interrupted brusquely. "I have been sitting in the saddle for twelve hours, and I ache all over. There is a wound I want my physician to attend to. So if you have something to say..." The Caliph rose, a tall, powerfully built man with the weather-beaten face of the seasoned soldier.

"Your Honor, that is precisely the matter I wish to speak of – the Jew who is your physician."

"My physician? And what concern of yours, may I ask, is my private doctor?" the Caliph asked in a dangerously quiet voice.

"I am not the only one who is concerned." Muhammed's eyes were like polished marbles, opaque, revealing nothing. "The court is concerned. Our great Muslim land is troubled."

"Indeed! Please proceed." The Caliph folded his arms and regarded his adviser with exaggerated patience.

"We have heard many questions, many complaints. People ask how this infidel, this vile nonbeliever – this Jew – could have gained the trust and confidence of our great ruler."

"How did he gain my trust? You really want to know?" The Caliph began to pace up and down the room in his heavy boots, bumping carelessly into the elegant tapestries and fine furniture. Each footstep was heavier than the last, the result of an old injury. "I trust him with my life and the lives of my children. And do you know why?" He stopped in front of Muhammed and waved an admonishing finger in his face. "Because he is honest and devoted. Because he wants nothing for himself. Influence, power, riches, they mean nothing to him. Nothing! The one thing he asks is to make life a little easier for his suffering brothers." The Caliph's craggy face softened a little, and he towered over his slender adviser. "Can any other officer in my court claim the same?"

"Your Majesty, I was afraid you would feel this way." The adviser pressed together the fingers of his slim and elegant hands.

He was silent for a moment, as if choosing his words carefully. "Your Majesty is aware that the war in the Holy Land keeps you out of the country much of the time, and the burden of rulership falls upon us. I would like to inform Your Majesty, in the name of the court, that we can no longer guarantee the stability of the crown in your absence."

"And what is all that supposed to mean?" the Caliph thundered.

"It means that your crown will be in great danger." The smooth, olive face was as inscrutable as ever.

The color of the Caliph's face deepened, until even his eyes seemed to darken from the rush of blood to his head. His large fist came crashing down on the table before him. "Are you threatening me?"

Muhammed did not answer. He merely spread his hands in a slight gesture of helplessness.

The Caliph was silent, pacing back and forth furiously. This was blackmail, pure and simple. He was threatened with rebellion, outright insurrection, if his demands were not met. But what could he do? Muhammed had gained too much influence, too much power. He could not fight a battle on two fronts simultaneously. He would have to give in to him until he returned triumphant from his conquest of the Holy Land. And then his chief adviser had better watch out!

The Caliph kicked the low table with such force that it went crashing against the wall. "All right," he growled, "what do you want from me?"

"Permission to kill him," Muhammed replied in a voice as cold as iron.

The Caliph sat down heavily. The fierce battle and the long day on the road were catching up with him. He rubbed his eyes wearily.

"I will take care of all the arrangements," Muhammed added with a tiny smile. "It will be done with the greatest discretion. Your Majesty will not have to watch the execution if it is too painful for him."

"I watched more men die yesterday than you have seen die in a lifetime," the Caliph said thickly. "It's not death that bothers me, it's treachery." He realized with bitter irony that he himself would now be a partner in a betrayal, however unwillingly. He would be sending his good friend the physician, who had saved his life more than once, into a trap he could never suspect.

Muhammed outlined his plan in the calm manner of a person organizing palace entertainment. Near the city gates was a lime pit, where a constant fire was maintained by an attendant well known to Muhammed. The attendant, who was both simple and obedient, would be ordered to seize the first person who approached him in the morning bearing a message from the Caliph, and throw him into the fire. It would be arranged that the first person to appear would be the Jew, Maimonides.

The Caliph listened with smoldering eyes. "And what if, by

some mistake, a pure-hearted Muslim should precede the Jew to the pit? Will he be burned instead?"

"Not at all, Your Majesty." The adviser's voice was positively cordial. "I have thought of that as well. We will make sure there is no chance for a mistake. We will order the Jew to go to the man at the pit and say the following words: 'Have you done as the Caliph commanded?' Those words will identify him beyond a doubt. And as soon as our lime burner will hear those words, he will... do his job. As I have told Your Majesty, he is both simple and obedient."

The Caliph turned his back on the adviser. "Enough. Do what you want. But one more word and I... I will find someone else to hurl into that pit," he said, throwing a black look over his shoulder.

Muhammed only smiled and bowed.

The Rambam was leaving the palace after dressing the Caliph's wound. It was not a serious one, just the grazing of a spear, but the Caliph had seemed weary and dispirited. He probably needed time and rest to recover from the horrors of the battlefield.

Muhammed, the Caliph's chief adviser, was waiting for him at the palace gate. "I have a message for you from the Caliph," he said politely; but there was a gleam in those cold eyes that troubled the Rambam. "You do not have to visit the palace tomorrow. You are to go instead, early in the morning, to the gate of the city, where the lime is burned. And you must ask the lime burner the following question: 'Have you done as the Caliph commanded?' And remember, it must be done immediately after sunrise."

The Rambam regarded him in silence for a moment, and there was no mistaking the look of gloating satisfaction in his eyes. There was no doubt the adviser was scheming again, for he was filled with as much hatred as he could hold. For once, however, the Rambam could not understand what the man stood to gain from sending him on so foolish an errand. Perhaps that was it; perhaps he meant to discredit him by making him ask a meaningless question of the half-wit at the lime pit. The Rambam gave a slight shrug. "Many are the thoughts in the heart of man," he murmured to himself, "but it is the counsel of the L-rd that endures."

"What? What are you mumbling?" the courtier asked sharply.

The Rambam only nodded and said, "I will follow your instructions."

The rising sun found the Rambam walking briskly to the *beit k'nesset*. He had chosen a small synagogue in a poor neighborhood where he would not be recognized. He would take his time and pray undisturbed, in quiet contemplation; afterward he would fulfill the Caliph's puzzling little errand. The rest of the morning would be free, gloriously free. He would not have to make the long, grueling journey to the palace, nor have to deal with Muhammed and his friends. He would slip quietly into his library where the work was piled high on his desk: inquiries, questions on *halacha*, appeals from troubled communities. At last he would have a few hours to answer those important letters before his patients were due to arrive.

The morning prayer was wonderful, containing something of a Shabbat flavor. He would have lingered on and studied for a while in the stillness of the little synagogue, but the morning sun was rising in the sky, throwing circles of light onto the tiled floor; and he had yet to do the Caliph's command. Reluctantly, the Rambam turned to go.

He found his way barred by a very young man, thin and shabbily dressed and obviously in a state of great excitement. His frayed turban was askew, and his expression was at once uncertain and fiercely determined. "Rabbi!" he cried as he accosted the Rambam. "You *are* a rabbi, aren't you?"

The Rambam nodded in the affirmative.

"Rabbi, a son was born to me."

"*Mazel Tov*, my son, and may you merit to raise him to Torah, to marriage, and to good deeds."

"Amen, amen, but first the rabbi must come to the *brit milah*. I have no one to circumcise him. No one would come to me, because I haven't got money to pay. You must come and help me," he finished desperately.

The Rambam stood undecided.

The young man locked his fingers together and tore them apart nervously. "What shall I do if I cannot enter my son into the covenant of our father Avraham? He is a Jewish child, isn't he?"

The simple question affected the Rambam deeply. Could such an appeal be denied? Whose command came first, the command of a man of flesh and blood, or the command of the King of the Universe? He would go quickly, help the young man fulfill the mitzva, and then hurry on to do the king's errand.

In the poor, little house at the edge of town, an attempt had been made at celebration. A white cloth was spread on the table, and a small bottle of wine and some flatbread lay in the center. The Rambam slipped some coins into the young father's hand and told him to send for all that was needed.

The tiny baby was lying on a clean white pillow, his two beautiful gray eyes gazing out intently from the small red face. A tender infant, already sanctified, already holy, would now enter the great and eternal covenant between him and the Creator of the world and His Chosen People.

The Rambam performed the mitzva with great feeling, reciting the blessing, "Blessed are You, oh L-rd, Who makes the covenant."

He took a little wad of cloth dipped in wine and slipped it into the baby's mouth. The infant immediately stopped crying and began to suck eagerly. "Oh, G-d and G-d of our fathers, preserve this child for his mother and his father, and let his name be called..."

"Yaakov," cried the father, his face radiant and triumphant, "Yaakov ben Naftali."

"May the father rejoice, and the mother rejoice, and she who bore you be glad." The pale young mother in the doorway was crying and smiling at the same time. For a moment the Rambam thought of his own young wife, cut off in her youth, and of the children they had not merited to raise. But this was a time for rejoicing. "Give thanks to the L-rd for He is good, for His kindness is everlasting."

The wine was strong and sweet. All around him were happy faces, warmth, comradeship, cries of *Mazal Tov*. It may have been the sudden respite from his tight schedule, from the constant exertion and vigilance that marked his days at the palace, but he did something he had never done before. In mid-morning the Rambam's eyes closed, and he slept.

He awoke with a start. The guests were dispersing. It must have been close to noon. He must hurry and do the Caliph's bidding.

The sun was high in the sky when he arrived at the gate. Great plumes of black smoke were rising from the malodorous pit. The man who burned the lime was a veritable giant, a great hulking figure covered with soot. Two fierce, little eyes glinted from his black face, and his expression was stupid and brutal. The Rambam had to remind himself that this too was a human being, a creation of the Almi-ghty.

"Have you done the Caliph's command?" he shouted over

the crackle of the flames.

The man dropped the shovel he was holding, placed his large, hairy hands on his stomach, and began to laugh in loud, piercing shrieks. His voice was surprisingly highpitched for his great size.

"Did I do what the Caliph commanded?" he yelled. "Yes, I did. I certainly did, even though he kicked up a big fuss. 'A mistake, a mistake,' he kept saying. But Amir makes no mistakes! The first man that comes and asks the right question, and it is done." He stood for a moment, a wide smile of reminiscence creasing his round, sootstreaked face. "He was a fine lord, no doubt about it, and he put up a good fight, kicking and scratching and threatening and begging. But in he went. Here I have proof." He bent down and held up a piece of green silk cloth, covered in ashes.

The Rambam stood still in amazement. It was the turban of Muhammed.

Amir tossed the turban at the Rambam and said, "Take it to the Caliph. Show him that Amir did it. He did what the Caliph commanded."

The Rambam leaned against the gate. Bit by bit the pieces began to fit together. "Tell me, Amir," he asked slowly, "what was it that the man in green asked you?"

"Why, the same as you did, sir. 'Did you do what the Caliph commanded?' But the difference is, you see, he was *first*." The half-wit's face was tense with concentration, and he frowned

*"Did I do what the Caliph commanded?"*

anxiously. "I did as I was told. I did right, didn't I?"

The Rambam nodded. "You did your job well."

As he walked aimlessly along after leaving the lime pit, he whispered to himself, "G-d watches those who love Him, and all the wicked He will destroy." A series of miracles had saved him from the flames of the pit: the mitzva of circumcision that had been placed in his path, his deep sleep in the middle of the morning. And these same miracles had brought upon Muhammed the destruction he had unwittingly created for himself! He had been unable to resist the temptation to see for himself if his plot had succeeded.

The Rambam shook his head. Much as the evil adviser had deserved his fate, it was a death one did not like to think about.

The Caliph stared wildly when he saw the Rambam. His eyes widened in horror, and he lurched clumsily to his feet. "It's all right, Your Majesty," the Rambam said, putting out a hand to steady him. "I am not an apparition."

The Caliph took a deep breath and sat down. Then a great smile spread slowly across his leathery face. "You scared me. Thank G-d, you are alive. Tell me how you escaped."

When the Rambam had finished explaining, the Caliph rose to his feet. "Blessed is your G-d and the G-d of your People," he said reverently. "He has saved the innocent and punished the wicked." Then a mottled redness darkened his face, and he dropped his eyes. "I guess I too have some explaining to do. You know that this plot was carried out with my permission."

"There must have been great pressure on the Caliph," said the Rambam tranquilly.

"Yes, yes, you see that, don't you?" asked the Caliph, anxiously. "He threatened me with an insurrection, a rebellion, while I was away at war. He knew my hands were tied – but it was wrong! It was wrong! One does not desert a comrade under fire."

He rose then and looked the Rambam squarely in the face. "But I swear to you now, it will never happen again. Never."

The Rambam only nodded and asked permission to examine the king. The wound was healing nicely; a few more days of rest, a change of bandages twice daily, and he would be ready to rejoin his troops.

Then he asked, "Your Majesty, may I speak a few words?"

"Of course," the Caliph replied, sitting at ease with his arms folded.

"You know that we Jews are commanded by the Torah to hold all life sacred, that we are forbidden to endanger, a human life – even our own?"

The Caliph nodded slowly.

"Your Majesty knows that this is not the first plot against me. According to the laws of the Torah I am forbidden to remain in a place where I have so many enemies. The Caliph would have to spend twenty-four hours a day guarding my life," he finished with a smile.

The Caliph was silent for a long moment. At last he sighed and said, "You are right, my friend. But where will you go? You are a prominent man. Wherever you go, your enemies will find you."

"I have been thinking about that," said the Rambam. "I think I will have to disappear for a while."

"Disappear?" asked the Caliph.

"I will find a hiding place for a few years. My enemies at court will eventually forget me and turn to other matters. I ask only one thing, Your Majesty – do not search for me."

"It will be as you wish," the Caliph replied sadly. "And may your great G-d continue to protect you."

"And I too will pray daily for your majesty's long life and continued success."

The Caliph rose to his feet, overcome by emotion. "That you should still... that you can wish me..." he stammered in a broken and muffled voice. "After all this... that you can forgive me and still wish me well!"

He grasped the Rambam's hands for a moment, and then with a great effort he mastered himself and continued. "I cannot do anything to repay you for all you have done for me. I cannot even offer you my protection. But one thing I *can* do. One day I will conquer the Holy Land and drive the Crusaders out of Yerushalayim. I promise you now that when the city is mine, I will establish there a haven for your People. I know how you feel

*" I will establish there a haven for your People."*

about your holy city and your scattered brothers. Let them come, from all corners of the world, and live undisturbed in their own land."

The Rambam's eyes shone radiantly. "Amein. May it be G-d's will."

All that was good and generous in the Caliph glowed in his strong face. "I will not forget."

## Chapter Fourteen

# THE CAVE

The large yeshiva hall was humming with the sound of Torah. Benyamin of Toledo wandered in, a visitor with some free time on his hands, seeking a place to learn. He smiled at the sight of the many young heads bobbing up and down to the chant of the Gemara. He too had once sat in such a room together with his good friend Moshe, swaying over the Talmud.

He listened and nodded and dropped some hints, and soon the bait was taken. Students sitting nearby turned around, others drifted over as he told them of his travels in Greece and Italy, Turkey, France, Germany, and Syria. He spoke of the many different Jewish communities that he had seen in his wanderings. The boys were fascinated by his account of an independent, warlike tribe, fearless and free, living in a stronghold in the mountains, governing themselves by the laws of the Torah.

The circle grew, the questions flew, and in the midst of it all the traveler looked about at his surroundings and asked casually, "This is the Rambam's yeshiva, isn't it? I knew him well in my youth. Hasn't he written a book?"

"A book?" There were cries of indignation at this question, and the eager young voices rivaled each other in praise of their teacher. "He has written many, many great works!"

"Haven't you studied his commentary on the Gemara? And what about his giant work on the entire Mishna?

"Haven't you seen the letters on *Kiddush Hashem*, written in his youth? And the letter to Yemen that saved an entire community in Israel?"

Benyamin of Toledo shook his head in wonder. "What a great man my old friend must have become. I knew him only as a boy in Toledo, but even then, he explained away all difficulties, removed all doubts. Even then, we all knew he had greatness in him, that he would be the teacher of all Israel."

The young heads nodded in agreement.

"You know, boys," he continued with a disarming smile, "I have come all this way to Egypt to see my old friend. Can any of you tell me his whereabouts?"

A sudden silence greeted the question, and all animation was wiped from the young faces. It was as though a screen had suddenly descended in front of the traveler. The students in the outer ring of the circle quietly slipped away; the others suddenly immersed themselves in their studies.

Rabbi Benyamin sighed. The reaction had been the same everywhere he had sought the Rambam. The entire Jewish community of Egypt seemed to be engaged in some giant conspiracy of silence. He saw a few of the boys exchange wary looks, apparently hiding some terrible secret. Only one hesitant young boy continued to stand before him, looking at him with searching eyes.

"Don't you see?" he appealed to the boy. "He is a friend of my youth. So few of us are left. We sat like this," he continued, pointing to two of the students who were swaying together. "Shall I leave without at least greeting him?"

The youth shook his head. "We are not allowed to tell! Why don't you speak to the *Rosh Yeshiva*?"

"Thank you, but I have tried that already." Benyamin smiled at the boy. "Don't be distressed. I am sure you all have a good reason for holding your silence. You boys certainly know how to keep a secret."

"Will you come again," asked the youth wistfully, "and tell us more about your travels?"

"G-d willing. I might even write a book."

Rabbi Benyamin walked down the pleasant streets. The branches of peach and date trees rustled overhead. It looked so peaceful, so prosperous, this Egypt of the Rambam. How could it have swallowed up his old friend, the famous physician and scholar, without a trace?

He was approaching an imposing building with a wrought-iron gate – the Rambam's home. It, too, had kept its secret. He had tried to enter it several times, but the discreet doorman with the brown face had informed him that the master of the house was away and that the family was receiving no visitors.

As he neared the house, he saw that the gate was moving.

A little girl with long black braids had her feet planted firmly on the iron bar and was swinging slowly back and forth, as an old Muslim nursmaid kept a close watch. The child had a distinctive little face, both delicate and strong. That high, white forehead... those intelligent, dark eyes, firm lips... where had he seen them before? Of course. It was a Maimon face. She must be his friend Moshe's little daughter.

He smiled. "You must be Rabbi Moshe's daughter."

"Oh, no. No, I'm not," she laughed. "Everybody thinks so, because I live here. I'm not his daughter. Uncle Moshe just takes care of us. I'm his niece." She let go of the gate with one hand and pointed to an upper window. "That's our apartment up there, where I live with my mother."

"You are Rabbi Moshe's niece," he repeated. "Why, then you must be... his younger brother David's little girl."

She nodded emphatically. "Yes, that's right. My father was my uncle's little brother. My mother told me that he went in a big ship in the middle of the ocean, and there was a great wind and it sank down, and never came up again." She told the story with the pragmatic acceptance of childhood, adding as an afterthought, "And his *neshama* is up in *Shamayim*."

So David had died young. They had been very close, the two brothers, and close to their father, the venerable *tzaddik* Rabbi Maimon. What a blow that must have been.

"Did you know him?" asked the child, slowing her swinging.

"Know whom?" he asked absently.

"My father."

"Yes, I did, years ago, when he was a little boy – not much older than you."

"Oh, tell me about him when he was little! My uncle tells me stories about him sometimes, but my mother says it makes him too sad."

Benyamin mused. "He was much younger than I was, but I used to see him with Rabbi Moshe. He was a nice little boy, with curly black hair and long eyelashes, a lot like yours. He was very bright, too, very studious. They used to learn everything together, your grandfather and the two boys, everything... Chumash, Mishna, and Gemara."

He stood hesitating, torn between conscience and the need to see his old friend. The child might know something. But would it be right to question her, to take advantage of such innocence? He too had daughters who were now grown. No, he would have to find another way.

But then the child surprised him. "Do you know where my uncle is?" she asked suddenly. "He went away. I'm not allowed to ask where he is, and I keep waiting and waiting, but he doesn't come back."

Benyamin's heart turned over. The lovely child had lost a father not once but twice. "Never fear, little one," he said gently. "Wherever he is, the Hashem is watching over him and guarding him from all harm."

He had pulled the right string, it seemed, for the little face beamed again. "That's what my mother says. Oh, look!" She pointed to a slender figure hurrying toward them. "That's my mother."

But the little girl spared him from having to explain. "Come, Mother, here is a rabbi who knew Father when he was little. Come and speak to him."

The young woman took her daughter's hand and said graciously, "Why don't you come in, sir? It is always good to hear from old friends."

Benyamin followed them into the courtyard, where a fountain splashed in the basin and peach blossoms lay scattered on the ground. He explained that he had come all the way from Toledo to visit his old friend, Rabbi Moshe, but had not been permitted to enter.

"Oh, yes," she sighed, and bit her lips. "It's for his safety. My brother-in-law... There are so many enemies. They have been sending spies. You see," she continued, looking up at him with tears in her eyes, "we are afraid. We don't know whom to trust."

He nodded. "I guessed as much. He is in hiding, then. I had hoped he was done with all the running and hiding, that here in Fostat..."

She shook her head. "Our people call him the Great Eagle. He has risen too high. Our enemies cannot bear it that a Jew should have such influence."

They spoke for a while about the past and about the tragic death of her husband. "But, thank G-d, I have my little girl. Rabbi Moshe has no one. The loss of his brother was a terrible blow to him. I don't know if he has yet recovered. It's such a pity that he can't see you. He talks often of the olden days, of Cordova and Toledo. It would be good for him to see an old friend."

Benyamin felt the awakening of hope. "Do you think that it would be possible for me to see him, even for a few moments?"

She sat quite still for a moment, thinking. "If you have a letter of recommendation..." she began hesitantly.

"Certainly," he said, reaching eagerly into his pocket, "from many rabbis..."

"No, no," she smiled. "It won't help to show them to me. You must meet with Rabbi Moshe's friend, Rav Yehudah HaCohen. He will check everything, and if he agrees... I do hope that you will be able to see him."

Three days later Rav Yehudah HaCohen, soft spoken man of slow and ponderous movements, scrutinized Benyamin's credentials. He shuffled the many letters of recommendation, murmuring, "The Ravad... aah, Rabbi Avraham ben David." He lifted heavy eyelids and nodded. "With this I am satisfied. We know we can trust you. But secrecy is of the essence. Not a word to anyone."

Benyamin nodded vigorously. "*Chas v'shalom* that I

should endanger my friend."

Rav Yehudah regarded him soberly. "Tomorrow a few students are going to visit him in his hiding place. Be outside the yeshiva after *Maariv*."

Benyamin rose, elated. He shook hands warmly with the dignified rabbi. "Thank you, thank you! You don't know what this means to me... after all these years."

The rabbi only nodded and laid a finger on his lips.

Two students were waiting for him the next evening in the black shadow of the yeshiva building. He followed them as they strode rhythmically through the darkened side streets leading to the outskirts of town.

They began to climb into the foothills outside of the city. The moon floated above the peaks, casting a pale sheen upon the path. Black masses of shadows lay all around them. The path grew steeper and then disappeared. The boys moved swiftly and surely, comfortably familiar with the trek.

Suddenly they halted. Benyamin glanced at his young guides in surprise. He saw nothing before him, only a rocky projection in the hillside, dimly illuminated by the phosphorescent glow of the moon. The boys peered sharply around them, then rapped several times loudly on the rock.

*What was this?* Benyamin wondered. *Some secret, underground path to the Rambam's hiding place?* Dumbly he watched as the students bent down, and with a sharp, scraping sound, pushed a boulder from the side of the cliff.

Benyamin instinctively stepped back when confronted with the intense, blinding light streaming out of the opening in the mountain. Then, blinking in amazement, he beheld the most awesome sight he had ever seen.

He was staring into a cave brightly lit by several tall, yellow wax tapers fixed to the veined rock wall. Behind a large desk strewn with rolls of parchment sat a Jew with a holy face that was framed by a silver beard. His entire being seemed to glow with some mysterious inner light.

For a wild moment, Benyamin thought he had stumbled upon the cave of the holy Rashbi, who had hidden from the Roman conquerors more than a thousand years ago.

The Rav behind the desk recognized him immediately. He rose with a kindly, welcoming smile and advanced toward his visitor with outstretched arms, crying, "Benyamin – from Toledo!"

It was then that the man realized that this rabbi was none other than his childhood companion Moshe, whom he had come to seek. But never again would he – could he – refer to his old friend in so familiar a manner...

Rabbi Moshe also greeted the two escorts, who had replaced the boulder and now stood silent and awed in the doorway. He thanked them for the packets and books they had brought and inquired after the health of his family and of his little niece.

*His entire being seemed to glow with some*
*mysterious inner light.*

Then he turned back to Benyamin and smiled. He questioned his friend closely about his life, his family, his travels through the lands of Jewish dispersion. He listened intently to Benyamin's account of the Jewish communities he had crossed in his wanderings.

Benyamin answered to the best of his ability, but at last he could contain himself no longer. "Rabbi Moshe, what are you doing here all alone, in this cave in the wilderness?"

He had expected to find the great Rambam in hiding, but not cramped in a rough hole and denied the most basic human comforts. He spotted a blanket on a cot in the corner and shuddered at the thought of this great man, no longer young, spending his nights alone in the chill of the desolate hills. "Couldn't they have found you a better place, a house...?"

The Rambam shook his head. "I am too well known to jeopardize the safety of a Jewish family by allowing them to hide me. Don't look so downcast," he added with a warm smile. "Believe me, my friend, it is all for the best. I have not known such peace and tranquility since my childhood in Cordova. Come, I will show you something."

Benyamin came closer, and Rabbi Moshe pointed to several rolls of parchment neatly arranged in a box on the large desk. "I have been working on a new book. Do you remember, Benyamin, when we were students together and you used to listen to my plans and dreams? I have been wanting to do this for a long time, but only now, through the workings of Divine

Providence, have I found the peace I needed to pursue this project. I wish to gather every law of the Torah, all the mitzvot drawn from the Oral Law, and lay them all before the student in plain language and a clear style. There shall be fourteen books in all."

Rabbi Moshe stood up, his eyes shining. "You see, I wish to organize the *halachot* according to their subject matter. To save the student weariness and confusion, all the mitzvot pertaining to one subject will be found in the same place. So when a student of the Gemara wishes to clarify a law – do you remember, Benyamin, how you struggled in those early years? – he will not have to search through all the Talmud. For who can remember the Talmud and all its laws by heart?"

"Only you," smiled Benyamin. "Yes, yes – what a fabulous undertaking! But it will take a lifetime. All the *halachot* in the Torah..." He shook his head in wonder. "If you would limit yourself, forgive me for saying so, to the laws that have practical application to our lives now, here in exile, it would be a reasonable task. But *all* the laws, Reb Moshe, even the laws of sacrifices, the harvesting of crops in the Holy Land..."

"*All* the laws, my friend," Rabbi Moshe repeated firmly. "Very soon our Redeemer will come, and we will be gathered from the four corners of the world. Soon we will rebuild our Holy Temple, and bring sacrifices on the altar, and harvest the crops of the land of Israel, and rest in the *Shemitta* year. We will need to be fully conversant in all the laws in the very near future."

His voice, always so calm and rational, was throbbing with a deep longing. "How will we fulfill these mitzvot in the days of Mashiach if we do not study them now? And in the merit of studying them, may we be granted to fulfill them, speedily in our day!"

"What will you call your book?" asked Benyamin.

The two young students leaned forward in eager anticipation. They felt privileged; they would be the first to know about the next great work of their teacher.

"I will call it '*Mishneh Torah*' – so that every Jew, once he has learned the written Torah, will be able to turn to this book to find help in fulfilling the mitzvot correctly and studying the Talmud with greater ease."

Benyamin sensed that despite all the cordiality on the face turned toward him, despite the patient reply to every question, the interview was over. The Rambam wished to be left alone to work on his great book. The fire of his dedication would keep him writing late into the night, filling the barren cave with the warmth and light of the Torah.

Benyamin and the two students walked home quietly together. A wonderful stillness hung in the air. The stars shone down, and their rays seemed to shed a great peace on the world.

The student with the searching eyes said quietly, "I feel as if I had just seen Rabbi Shimon Bar Yochai in his cave, with Eliyahu Hanavi teaching him Torah."

Many years later, Benyamin heard a marvelous sequel to the scene he had just witnessed.

For ten years the Rambam labored on his great work. When he had completed it, he fell into a deep sleep and had a dream. He saw his father enter the cave, together with a man dressed all in white whose face shone with an extraordinary radiance. "I have come to you, my son," said Rabbi Maimon, "and here with me is Moshe Rabbeinu."

"Moshe Ben Maimon," said the man with the radiant face, "I have come to see the book you have written."

He walked over to the pile of manuscripts and examined them for a few moments. Then, turning to the Rambam, he added solemnly, "Well done, Moshe Ben Maimon."

## Chapter Fifteen

# THE EUROPEAN VISITORS

Avraham stood up respectfully when the visitors entered the dining room. His father had taught him that one must conduct oneself with humility and courtesy toward every human being created in the image of G-d; how much more so toward a Jew and a scholar.

Avraham was a slight boy of eleven, frail and small for his age, but his face, both sensitive and alert, bore an expression older than his years. He was the only surviving child of the Rambam, born after those years in hiding, and the boy had spent many hours in the company of his illustrious father. Rabbi Moshe guided his son's education with the most exacting and tender care. He allowed him to be present at many meetings and interviews with people from all walks of life. Avraham knew his father had great hopes for him, a knowledge that filled him with an equal measure of joy and trepidation. Learning how to understand people, to deal with them wisely and kindly, was as much a part of his training as were the holy books that he studied.

Now the young boy turned his bright, inquisitive gaze upon the visitors. The rabbi from France was a tall, broad man with fair skin, burned pink from the sun, and a bushy auburn beard. He was dressed in black from head to toe, as was the young student who accompanied him, and his restless blue eyes moved uneasily from the colorful mosaics on the wall to the patterned carpet.

The Rambam greeted his guests graciously, inviting them to be seated and to refresh themselves after their rigorous journey. The older visitor gazed down in perplexity at the low table, spread with bowls of fruit and nuts and decorated with bright red mandrake flowers; then his glance wandered to the large silk pillows arranged on the floor. Very slowly and awkwardly, he lowered his heavy frame to the floor. The young student at his side followed suit, tucking his long thin legs under him with far more agility.

"You will excuse us, Rabbi Meir," the Rambam said, smiling at his guests. "I know the customs of dining in our Eastern lands differ from your own." During the meal, he inquired about their long journey over sea and desert. The rabbi from France answered rather shortly that it had been strenuous but that all had gone well, *Baruch Hashem*. The Rambam guided the conversation to Rabbi Meir's homeland and its great rabbis and yeshivot, whose fame had spread throughout the world.

"Have you learned, perhaps, with the great scholar and commentator, Rabbi Avraham ben David?" he asked.

The young student remained humbly silent, but Rabbi Meir answered stiffly that he had indeed had the privilege of learning Torah at the feet of Rabbi Avraham ben David.

"Why was this visitor from France so distant and

unfriendly?" Avraham wondered. Most Jews who were granted the privilege of dining with the Rambam were brimming with awe and gratitude. Then he remembered the conversation he had had with his father several weeks earlier.

"We are having visitors from Ashkenaz," his father had told him, glancing up from a letter. "Rabbi Meir from France."

"All that way," Avraham had marveled, "just to learn Torah from you, Father!"

Rabbi Moshe had shaken his head, and a sad smile had touched his face. "No, not exactly, Avraham. More likely to examine me, I fear."

Avraham had been quite perplexed. How would anyone dare to examine the Rambam?

But his father had not answered him. "Don't worry, my son, all will be well, all will be clarified, with Hashem's help."

Now Avraham puzzled over the cryptic visit again. Examine the Rambam? Examine his father, who was the leader of Jewish people the world over, who was called "The Great Eagle," "The Light of the East and the West?" Even the Muslims regarded him with awe, and the Caliph himself sought his advice. Important letters from every land lay piled high in baskets in his office. Even when his father had been sick, unable to lift his head from the pillow, he had dictated answers to his students, knowing that his help was so urgently needed.

"Please serve our guests, Patrus," Rabbi Moshe said

pleasantly to the tall, angular man who stood a few paces behind him. Patrus was never far from his master's side; he was not just a servant, but a disciple and unofficial guard. His dark, watchful face was turned protectively toward the Rambam, prepared to respond instantly to the slightest gesture.

He moved forward on silent feet and lifted the large silver bowl from the center of the table. Avraham saw that a rare delicacy had been prepared for the visitors, a vegetable with delicate rootlike stalks that were both delicious and – his father had told him – very nutritious. Patrus bent forward and offered the vegetable first to the head of the house and then to the visitors.

Rabbi Meir looked at the bowl before him, and a strange thing happened. His blue eyes opened wide, a shudder seemed to go through him, and his ruddy face was drained of all color.

"Excuse me..." he murmured in a shaky voice, shutting his eyes for a moment, "the long journey... I am not at all hungry."

The young student at his side also closed his lips tightly and shook his head. The Rambam cast a sharp glance at his visitor but said nothing. After that, the conversation lagged.

"Patrus," Rabbi Moshe said at last, "our visitors are weary from their travels. Perhaps a bit of strong, sweet wine from the cellar will revive them."

Once again, Rabbi Meir started violently. He gazed with a look of utter confusion from Rabbi Moshe to Patrus and back again. Then he said weakly, "No, thank you... no wine for me.

Cold water is all I need." His companion nodded in vigorous agreement.

Rabbi Meir asked permission to recite the *Birchat Hamazon* and retire, explaining that he hadn't realized how tired he was. Rabbi Moshe nodded pleasantly and said he would join him. As the visitor struggled wearily to his feet, the Rambam raised his voice slightly and said to Patrus, "Do me one more favor, Patrus. Do not forget to kill the little calf in the barn. It will provide a refreshing meal for our guests when they have recovered from their journey."

Avraham was certain that the remark was intended for the visitors from Ashkenaz. And indeed, Rabbi Meir spun around in the doorway and stared at his host with a look of helpless horror. Then, stumbling a little, he blundered out of the room in a great hurry, his companion close behind him.

Avraham sought his father's eyes. But Rabbi Moshe was stern and preoccupied, and a slight frown passed over his face. Then he smiled a weary sort of smile and shook his head.

"Father, what is the matter with our guests?" Avraham asked timidly.

His father put a reassuring hand on his shoulder. "They are quite perplexed, Avraham, but no matter. Tomorrow, G-d willing, all will be clarified."

Avraham certainly hoped so. The behavior of the rabbi from France was a deep mystery to him. He was certain that they were not merely tired; something had happened at the dinner table that had shocked and horrified them, and no matter how hard he tried, Avraham could not solve the puzzle.

Right after *Shacharit*, Avraham hurried to the study. His father did not have to leave for the Caliph's palace right away, and such mornings were always a treat.

The Rambam was grave and thoughtful, as he had been the night before, but his face softened when he saw his son. "I would like you to stay with me, Avraham, because you may learn something this morning. We must watch ourselves, my son, we who consider ourselves scholars and pious Jews. We must guard ourselves from arrogance and pride. We might easily come to the conclusion that there is only one way to serve the Alm-ghty – *our* way. And then how easy it becomes to judge our fellow Jews and condemn them hastily."

He sighed a little, lost in thought, and then added, "Remember, my Avraham, Torah is like water. It flows *downward* – to those who are contrite and lowly in spirit." There was a knock on the door, and Patrus appeared with the two visitors behind him. If anything, Rabbi Meir looked more exhausted than he had the night before. His eyes were red-rimmed and puffy, his face haggard and pale.

The Rambam regarded them with a steady gaze for a few seconds and then said, "My friends, I regret that you have not spent a restful night in my home and that you were unable to share our meal last night. I realize you have been troubled by some questions, some... doubts. I would appreciate it if you would speak up openly and without fear."

Rabbi Meir cleared his throat and glanced questioningly at Avraham.

"I would like my son to stay with me, if it is agreeable to you," the Rambam requested.

Rabbi Meir nodded, cleared his throat again, and began. "Honored Rav, we are strangers in this land. We know our customs differ, and perhaps, too, our ways of deciding the halacha..."

"Rabbi Meir," the Rambam's quiet voice cut in, "what upset you at our meal last night?"

"Rabbi Moshe, I will tell you the truth. The first dish we were served was so shocking, so strange! It looked – it looked – it seemed to me at the time that it was a... a human hand."

The young student nodded in agreement.

Avraham stared in disbelief at the two men. A human hand? Did they really imagine...?

Behind him he heard a sudden, sharp sound, quickly cut off. Was Patrus laughing? No, his dark face was impassive as ever.

"Avraham," said the Rambam, "what was the food in the silver bowl that we served last night?"

"Oh, that!" Avraham could no longer contain himself and burst into peals of laughter. "That wasn't a hand, it was a vegetable that grows here in Egypt. We serve it only on special occasions..."

Rabbi Meir dropped his eyes and stared at his large white hands which lay folded on the desk. The strong color flooded upward from his reddish beard to the fair, curly hair that had escaped from his black hat. "It was my mistake," he murmured. "But the wine, Rabbi Moshe – how do you explain the wine?"

"And what troubled you about the wine?"

"Why, Rabbi Moshe," Rabbi Meir replied in a trembling voice, "you asked your Muslim servant here to pour it. In Ashkenaz we are very particular even about wine that has been seen, never mind touched, by a non-Jew."

The Rambam's voice was so low that they had to bend forward to hear him. "Rabbi Meir, did you really believe that I would serve you wine that our sages had forbidden? Patrus, tell our guests who you are," he added, turning to his servant.

"I am Patrus, the son of Eliezer." Patrus glared at the visitors, but Avraham guessed that he was more annoyed at these strange Jews for causing his master aggravation than because of the slur on his ancestry.

"Are you a Jew, my son?"

"And my father before me."

"It was the name that misled you, among other things," the Rambam explained in his steady, controlled voice. "But Patrus is mentioned in the Talmud; if you will recall, 'Rabbi Yosef, the son of Patrus.'"

The two nodded slowly.

"And last of all, I am sure you would both like to know about the calf I ordered Patrus to kill. You want to know how I could dispense with the laws of *shechita*. I must confess that when I saw how deeply you mistrusted me, how ready you were to believe the worst, I couldn't resist testing you. Do you really think that I would have served you meat that was not kosher?"

Once again the Rambam turned to his faithful servant for assistance in explaining the *halachic* puzzle to his visitors. "Tell them about our little calf, Patrus."

"The calf was found in the womb of its mother, after the butcher had slaughtered her," said Patrus, still glowering at the visitors.

"And such a calf, Rabbi Meir–" Rabbi Moshe prompted him. "Does not need *shechita*. It has fulfilled the requirement through the *shechita* of its mother."

Rabbi Meir did not lift his eyes from his lap for some time. At last, when he seemed to have gathered resolution, he rose to his feet and looked straight into the Rambam's. "Rabbi Moshe, I owe you an apology. Please pardon my unforgivable behavior and my completely unfounded suspicions, and especially for failing to honor a Torah giant like yourself."

"To forgive is easy. I forgive you with all my heart," Rabbi Moshe said gently. "But as yet I do not understand. We have all learned that we must judge our fellow Jews favorably, and that before we incriminate them we must search scrupulously. So I must ask myself, what is it that could have predisposed these scholars and G-d-fearing men to suspect me of things that one does not normally suspect in a fellow Jew? In short, my friends, I am asking what it is that the learned rabbis in Ashkenaz have heard about me. What is my sin and my wrongdoing?" the Rambam finished with a soft smile.

Rabbi Meir took a deep breath. "I will be frank with you, Rabbi Moshe, since it is no use hiding anything from your eyes. It is your book, *Moreh Nevuchim – The Guide to the Perplexed.* Those who have read it..."

"I take it you have not," interposed the Rambam.

"No, I was afraid that – well, I was told..." he stammered.

"That it might turn you away from the true path," Rabbi Moshe finished for him drily. "So tell me, Rabbi Meir, what has upset the rabbis about this book?"

"You see, Rabbi Moshe, there is much written in this book about Greek philosophy and about Aristotle. The rabbis feel that in some places you seem to say that Torah and philosophy are equal, that the truth can be found in both, that there is no real difference between them."

Rabbi Moshe sat quite still, and his face seemed carved in stone; then suddenly, he sprang to his feet. "No difference between them? Is that what you said?"

Avraham had never seen his father so angry before, and the dark eyes that blazed like burning coals in his pale face unsettled him.

"Is there a difference between light and dark?" the Rambam continued in a formidable tone. His hands gripped the desk until his knuckles showed white. "The holy and the profane? The words of Eternal G-d and those of feeble man?"

The two men had stepped back instinctively, as if stung by the force of his anger. He looked at their frightened faces and then, with a small sigh, sat down, passing a hand across his forehead. Patrus moved closer, ever vigilant of his master's health since his recent illness; but Rabbi Moshe reassured him with a nod.

"Believe me," he began in a low voice, "nothing has caused me so much pain – not the plots of my enemies, not the envy of foolish people – nothing has ever hurt me as much as knowing that the great rabbonim of France, my fellow scholars, could believe...

"Listen, my friend," he resumed after a moment, turning once again to Rabbi Meir, "I do not boast that I have never made a mistake. Show me that I am wrong and I will change what I have written! But all I ask is that you read what I have written. Do not ascribe to me things that I have never said.

"I have listed the principles of faith. Have you read them? The belief in One G-d, eternal and unchanging, the Creator of all things, the belief in Divine Providence, in Torah from Heaven, in the coming of Mashiach. Tell me, is that Greek philosophy? Are those the beliefs of Aristotle?"

Rabbi Meir had been standing silently throughout this

speech, his head sunk onto his chest. At last he lifted his face, and Avraham saw that it was wet with tears. "Tell me one thing, Rabbi Moshe," he said in a broken voice, "how did the scholars of France come to make such a mistake?"

"I will tell you, my son." The Rambam's face was once again kind and gentle. "This book was not written for everyone. I wrote it for a student of mine, a fine, sincere young man who had studied too much philosophy. In his heart, in the depths of his soul, he was bound to Torah and the truth of our Faith, but his mind was filled with doubt and confusion. In the book, I tried to show him and other confused people like him that the Torah of Hashem is true and eternal. Don't you see," he asked in appeal, "that I had to use the language of philosophy, a language they understood and respected, to teach them the truth of our faith?"

"Rabbi Moshe, in the name of the rabbis of Ashkenaz," Rabbi Meir said in a trembling voice, "I beg your forgiveness for doubting a great man in Israel..."

"I forgive you with all my heart," said Rabbi Moshe warmly. "And now tell me what else is troubling you."

"No, no, no." Rabbi Meir stepped back. It was clear he had had enough. "This was our main question; the rest is a much less significant matter."

"Rabbi Meir, speak." the Rambam replied in a commanding voice. "You were sent on a mission. You are duty-bound to fulfill it."

Rabbi Meir sighed and drew a deep breath. "This question

is about the *Mishneh Torah*," he said apologetically. "Believe me, Rabbi Moshe, this book is honored and revered. It is called the *Efod*, the breastplate of Aharon which answers all questions."

"But..." prompted Rabbi Moshe.

"Only one thing troubles our *rabbonim*. You have set forth the completed halacha, the final verdict of the Gemara. You tell us the mitzvot that we should keep. But you do not explain the reasons for your decisions. So a rabbi like Rabbi Avraham ben David cannot be sure if he agrees with you since he does not know the source of your conclusions."

"Rabbi Avraham ben David is correct," the Rambam said simply. "The complaint of the rabbis is justified. I will rectify it and add in each case the reasons for my conclusion... If only Hashem will grant me health and time," he added softly.

Avraham looked up at his father in wordless wonder. How kind he was, and how forgiving! He did not know what it meant to bear a grudge.

He remembered words of Torah that he had been taught, and thought how appropriate they were for his own father, the Moshe of another generation:

*And G-d saw that we were weak and helpless,*

*And Moshe lifted his staff of strength and wisdom*

*Over the sea of confusion and error*

*And Israel crossed the sea on dry land*

*And he gave the Torah into their hearts.*

# Epilogue:

# GATES OF WISDOM

He must have been sleeping when the old man entered, because when Rabbi Moshe opened his eyes, he found the visitor standing beside his bed. Somehow the man had evaded the vigilant Patrus, who always guarded his master's room against intruders.

It was a very old Jew who stood before him, his face a network of wrinkles above his long white beard. His caftan was dusty from the road, and his gnarled hand rested on a heavy staff.

The Rambam struggled to sit up and greet the venerable old man, but a wave of weakness pressed him back against the pillow.

"Do not disturb yourself," the old man said in a voice deep and tranquil. "I see that you are not well. May Hashem grant you a speedy recovery." He looked deeply into the worn face on the pillow and seemed to sense what Rabbi Moshe already knew. He sighed a little and said, "So the wings of the Great Eagle have grown weary at last."

The visitor's eyes were blue, a blue as pure as the morning sky. Immediately, Rabbi Moshe felt that he could trust this old man completely – that he would understand. The old man sat down near his bed, and Rabbi Moshe told him what was in his heart.

"I am not complaining, *chas v'shalom*," he began. "G-d has granted me seventy years. And in my old age He blessed me with a son, who has brought only joy to his mother and to me. But look" – He pointed to the baskets, piled high with letters, which sat on the low table near the bed. "So many appeals for help, so much suffering. Here in the East, the Karaites are sapping our strength from within. Very few still learn Torah as it ought to be learned. In the West, thank G-d, yeshivot are flourishing, but the hatred and persecution our brothers face there is worse than anything we have yet seen. How can I tell them that my strength is gone, that they can no longer rely on me?"

"Rabbi Moshe ben Maimon," protested the old man, "they will always, always rely on you."

The Rambam did not answer. Tears were streaming down his face, and he had no strength to wipe them away.

"A faithful shepherd does not desert his flock," the visitor continued, his compassionate blue eyes seeming to glow in the dimness of the room. "Your light will shine upon them, Rabbi Moshe, more than ever. The Torah you have taught them will light their way to the coming of Mashiach."

"And Mashiach is still not here," whispered Rabbi Moshe.

"But he is, Rabbi Moshe. He is."

Suddenly, Rabbi Moshe was frightened. Had he been mistaken? Was the old man with the pure eyes an impostor, another false prophet to mislead his people? He struggled to raise himself from the pillow. But the old man laid his hand gently on Rabbi Moshe's heart.

"Here, Rabbi Moshe. Deep in the innermost sanctuary of a Jewish soul there is a place where exile has no power, where G-d rules alone. And a holy temple stands there, just as it is written, 'And I will dwell within you' – meaning that G-d will dwell within the *neshama* of every Jew."

Rabbi Moshe understood at last. "You are a Kabbalist," he said reverently.

The old man nodded.

"To reveal the inner light," mused Rabbi Moshe, "to penetrate the innermost secrets of our holy Torah. I have often wished... if there had only been time. But now it's too late." He shook his head regretfully.

"But that is why I have been sent to you," smiled the old man.

"Sent to me?"

"Yes, I have been sent to you from the holy city of Yerushalayim, Rabbi Moshe ben Maimon, to teach you the wisdom of the Kabbalah."

"But why to me?"

The old man turned his palms upward. "That I do not

know. Perhaps this is your reward for having toiled so long and so faithfully to clarify the *halacha* and to teach our People the mitzvot of Hashem."

A quiet happiness filled Rabbi Moshe's heart. "Is it not too late?" he asked. Will you take me into the *Pardes*? Will you reveal to me the hidden treasures of our Torah?"

"With Hashem's help," replied the old man quietly. "But you yourself, Rabbi Moshe ben Maimon, have already uncovered many treasures – more, perhaps, than you know. When you wrote your great book, the *Mishneh Torah*, G-d's spirit rested upon you. And how did your book begin? *'The foundation of foundations and the pillar of wisdom.'* The beginning letters of each of these words form the Holy Name of G-d, *Yud Kay, Vov Kay*. Did you know that this Name contains within it the secret of Creation?"

Rabbi Moshe sat up in bed. A new strength seemed to flow through him.

"And how did you end your *Mishneh Torah*?" continued the old man. "*'And the earth will be filled with the knowledge of G-d, as the water covers the sea'* – referring to the days of Mashiach. There you touched upon the Ultimate Revelation. For then we will see with our own eyes that there is no one and nothing besides Him, that nothing exists except the Holy One, Blessed Be He, and we will know then that this physical world is not a thing apart from G-d, but that it, too, is holy. It, too, is G-dliness."

Rabbi Moshe was leaning forward, drinking in every word. For a moment, he was back in his father's study, with David beside him, diving into a sparkling new world of comprehension. His face was pale as parchment, his beard white as snow; but his eyes were the shining eyes of the small boy who had found the gates of wisdom opening before him.

# Important Dates and Events
# in the Life of the Rambam*

**4895 (4893)(4898)**    14th of Nissan, The Rambam is bom in Cordova, Spain.

**4908**    The Maimon Family flees Cordova to escape persecution at the hands of the Almohades.

**4918 (4921)**    The Rambam begins writing his commentary on the Mishna.

**4919**    The Maimon Family flees to Fez, Morocco.

**4922**    The Rambam writes *Iggeret HaShmad.*

**4924 (4925)**    The Maimon family travels to Eretz Yisrael.

**4925 (4928)**    The Rambam completes his commentary on the Mishna.

**4926**    Rabbi Maimon, father of the Rambam, passes away. The family settles in Egypt.

**4927 (4930)**    The Rambam begins writing *Sefer HaMitzvot* and the *Mishneh Torah.*

**4929**    He writes and sends *Iggeret Taiman* to the Jews of Yemen.

**4931**    Rabbi David ben Maimon, brother of the Rambam, drowns in a shipwreck.

**4937**    The Rambam is appointed Chief Rabbi by the Cairo Jewish community.

**4946**    28th of Sivan, birth of Rabbi Avraham, son of the Rambam.

**4964**    The Rambam completes *Moreh Nevuchim.* 20th of Tevet Rabbi Moshe ben Maimon passes away and is buried in Tiberias, Israel.

* Where dates are in dispute by historians, alternatives appear in parenthesis.

# Glossary

Due to the geographical setting of the story, all Hebrew words have been transliterated using the Sephardic pronunciation.

Abba-Father

Al Kiddush Hashem - For the sanctification of G-d's name

Almohades - Fanatic Muslim sect

Amar Rava - Rava taught

Ana Hashem - "Please, O G-d!"

Anusim - Jews who were forced to convert; Marranos

Ashkenaz - Germany; of European origin

Ashrei Yoshvei Veitecha - "Happy are those who dwell
in Your tent" -a Psalm

Avraham Avinu - Abraham our Father

B'nei Yisrael - The Children of Israel

Bet Din - A Jewish court

Beit HaMikdash - The Holy Temple

Beit Hillel - The School of Hillel

Beit K'nesset - Synagogue

Beit Shammai - The School of Shammai

Bar Mitzva - Literally "a son of the commandments."
- At the age of 13 a boy becomes obligated to keep
the Torah's commandments.

Birchat Hamazon - Grace after Meals

Bimah - The podium in the synagogue

Birchat Hagomel - Blessing recited upon being delivered
from danger

Baruch Dayan Haemet - "Blessed is the True Judge" - recited
upon receiving news that someone has passed away

Baruch Hashem - Blessed is G-d

Brit Milah - Circumcision

Chavrusa - Learning partner

Chol Hamoed - Intermediary days of a holiday

Chumash - The Five Books of Moses

Dayan-Judge

Eliyahu Hanavi - Elijah the Prophet

Eretz Yisrael - The Land of Israel

Erev Pesach - The day before Passover

Etrog - Citron used on the Holiday of Sukkot

Galut - Exile

Gan Eden - The Garden of Eden

Gemara - The Talmud, the Oral Law of the Torah

Get - Divorce document

Geula - Redemption

Goy - Non-Jew

Halacha - Jewish law

Hashem - G-d

Kaddish - Prayer for the deceased

Karaites - a heretical sect of Jews who rejected the Oral Torah

Kashrut - Laws of keeping kosher

Kotel - short for Kotel Hamaaravi, the Western Wall

L' shana Haba'ah - Next year

Lulav - Palm branch used on Succos

Maariv - Evening prayer service

Marranos - Spanish Jews who secretly kept their faith while pretending to embrace the beliefs of the church

Mazal Tov - Good luck; congratulations

Mezuza - Parchment scroll containing the *Shema* prayer which is hung on the doorpost

Mikdash M'at - Small sanctuary

Mincha - Afternoon prayer service

Mishna - Compilation of Oral Law

Mitzva - One of 613 Divine commandments

Modeh Ani - Prayer recited upon awakening, thanking G-d for returning one's soul

Moshe Rabbeinu - Moses

Mashiach - The Messiah

Neshama - Soul

Nissan - Jewish month in which Passover occurs

Pardes - Orchard; acronym for *Pshat, Remez, Drush,* and *Soad* - various levels of Torah interpretation.

Parsha - Portion of the Bible

Pirkei Avot - Ethics of the Fathers, part of the Mishna

Pasuk - Verse

Rabbi Akiva - Great Torah scholar who lived at the time of the destruction of the Second Temple

Rabbi Shimon Bar Yochai - Outstanding student of Rabbi Akiva, revealed profoundest secrets of the Torah

Rabbi Yehudah Hanasi - Compiler of the Mishna

Rabbanim - Rabbis

Rachel Imeinu - Rachel, our mother

Rambam - Rabbi Moshe ben Maimon, known as Maimonides

Ravad - Rabbi Avrohom ben David, contemporary of the
Rambam, a great scholar and commentator

Ribono Shel Olam - Master of the Universe

Rosh Yeshiva - Head of a yeshiva

Seder - Ritual retelling of the story of the Exodus from
Egypt on Passover

Sedarim (of Gemara) - Sections of the Talmud

Sefer - Holy book

Sefer Torah - Torah scroll

Shabbat - The Sabbath

Shacharit - The morning prayer service

Shamash - Caretaker of a synagogue

Shechita - Ritual way to slaughter an animal

Shema Yisrael - "Hear O Israel"

Shiur - Torah lesson

Shiva - Seven-day mourning period

Shmonah Esrei - The Eighteen Benedictions, silent prayer

Shofar - Ram's horn

Shomer Chinam - An upaid guardian

Shomer Sachir - A paid guardian

Siddurim - Prayer book

Sifrei Torah - See Sefer Torah

Succot - Festival of Booths

Succah - Booth in which all meals are eaten during Succos

Tallit - Prayer shawl

Talmid Chacham - Torah scholar

Talmud - Compendium of Oral Law

Tefillin - Phylacteries

Tefillot - Prayers

Tehillim - Psalms

Torah - The Five Books of Moses

Tzaddik - Righteous man

Yerushalayim - Jerusalem

Yeshiva - Jewish school of learning

Yom Tov - Festival

Zecher Tzaddik L'vracha - May his memory be blessed
(said of a righteous person)

This book is based on real historical events, places, quotations,
and dates from the life of the Rambam.
However, certain conversations, characters,
and incidents are fictional.